Perspectives

On Planting Pride

By Marvin N. Miller, Ph.D.

Thoughtful reflections and impressions of
gardening, life, and
current research in the field of horticulture
and how it affects
communities and individuals.

Perspectives

On Planting Pride

By Marvin N. Miller, Ph.D.

ISBN-13: 978-1500850036

ISBN-10: 1500850039

America in Bloom® is a registered trademark.

Printed in USA 2014

America in Bloom® envisions communities across the country as welcoming and vibrant places to live, work, and play – benefiting from colorful plants and trees; enjoying clean environments; celebrating heritage; and planting pride through volunteerism.

Concept, editing, design and layout courtesy Evelyn Alemanni, www.allea.com.

www.americainbloom.org

Additional copies of this book are available at

www.americainbloom.org and Amazon.com.

Forward

By Charlie Hall, AIB President

Following in the footsteps of a giant is never easy. That is exactly what I am attempting to do as AIB's current president. As many of you know, Marvin served as AIB's president for many years, leading AIB through the trials and tribulations of a volunteer organization. I use the word "giant" on purpose – for what Marvin may lack in vertical stature, he makes up in heart, and his heart is as gigantic as Texas (the place I call home so I should know!). He has shared that heart with countless individuals in his role as president of AIB for many years and, undoubtedly, that impact is going to continue to be felt for years to come.

Someone once defined a volunteer as doing the good you can, by all the means you can, in all the ways you can, in all the places you can, at all the times you can, to all the people you can, as long as you ever can. I like that definition and as I pondered it, I thought it perfectly described Marvin and his style of leadership. For though he may not serve as president of the organization, he is still very much involved as past president and will likely, ceteris parabis, continue well into the future through AIB committee involvement.

In his day job, Dr. Miller is an economist and widely recognized hortistician (short for horticultural statistician). In this role, he must communicate numbers and theories in a manner that is both understandable and entertaining to audiences both within Ball Horticultural Company and across the green industry at large. This is no easy task. But Marvin is also a plant lover and recalls fondly early childhood memories of standing with his father amidst tomato plants. Plus, anyone who has seen his personal garden can attest that he practices what he preaches.

It is from these perspectives that Marvin has shared his thoughts, musings, and factoids with the AIB audience through his president's column in the AIB monthly newsletter. These are what are captured in this volume. There are some real nuggets of truth and wisdom contained within these pages and I, along with you, look forward to recalling them. Enjoy the reading!

Forward

About this Book

For nearly 10 years (2005 - 2014) Dr. Marvin N. Miller served as America in Bloom's president. During that time, America in Bloom's monthly newsletter included his thoughts on matters related to the organization and its participants–ranging from community involvement, the power of volunteers, to trees, flowers, horticultural research, and much more. These heartfelt epistles, written from a passion for horticulture and America in Bloom, offer ideas to ponder, share, and reflect. Although they were written between 2008 and 2014, the messages are timeless and will become richer on re-reading.

In this volume, we have collected all of these writings that we could find and hope you will enjoy Dr. Miller's insights into what can, and will, make American communities great. They are presented with the most recent first.

About America in Bloom

America in Bloom connects people to plants at a grassroots level through education and participation. Founded in 2001, America in Bloom was awarded the American Horticultural Society's 2009 Urban Beautification Award. This prestigious award is given to an individual, institution, or company for significant contributions to urban horticulture and the beautification of American cities.

Each year, since 2002, America in Bloom has presented a national awards program for best quality of life in American cities. What sets this program apart from other awards programs is that a team of specially trained, qualified judges visits each participant for two days, then they write a detailed evaluation that provides a roadmap for future enhancements. The program is based on achievements in four key areas: environmental awareness, heritage preservation, horticulture, and community involvement. While the program is holistic, encompassing the many facets that enhance quality of life, America in Bloom cities know that flowers, trees, shrubs, turf, and groundcovers of the right kind in the right place make a visual impact. Our cities know the economic importance of having their main streets landscaped, as they serve as the welcome signs inviting folks to spend time in the city. They know that well-maintained parks are good, not just for a healthy environment, but for healthy citizens. Communities also realize that these efforts are enhanced by attention to overall impression, environment, and heritage preservation.

To do all these things requires the synergy that comes from an engaged, and empowered, active community which combines the efforts of municipal and business partners working in cooperation with residents. The phenomenon of the "AIB bug" that infects people who have become involved with the program is palpable. Once citizens experience the true community spirit that results when everyone pitches in to make visible improvements, there is often no turning back. Indeed, a number of city administrations have attempted to cut back on beautification efforts or community enhancements only to face voters' wrath at the next election. Residents come to relish the community as it has been transformed.

America in Bloom has been credited with performing an impressive list of miracles in city after city nationwide. Mayor after mayor has told us the story of how America in Bloom has brought their city together like never before. Having municipal efforts working with business and organizational efforts and with those of residents, in concert, is often a first for many cities, but that's exactly what happens when America in Bloom comes to town. Mayors tell us of "a city transformed," and of "a more beautiful city." Often times the beautification efforts are surpassed only by the community enhancement aspects of the program.

Volunteers

Volunteers are the sustaining heartbeat and lifeblood of cities and towns. America in Bloom galvanizes volunteers from all walks of life, providing a framework for enhancing communities. Volunteers come from every demographic, every age group, schools, service groups, Scouts, churches, and business associations, who join in bringing communities together, creating a synergy of positive efforts with the joy of collaboration for permanent improvements.

Mayors have told us time after time that America in Bloom is the best community-building tool they've ever experienced; through participation in the program, all sectors have collaborated for the first time. That's the lasting power of America in Bloom.

Our judges and board of directors are all volunteers. Far more exciting is contemplating the countless volunteer hours donated in each of our participating cities. In Fayetteville, AR, one out of every three residents volunteers. In Bloomington, IN, 438 members of the Retired and Senior Volunteer Program donated 81,873 hours at 58 nonprofit organizations. One year, Logan, OH, tracked volunteer hours and tallied more than 100,000 donated hours.

That's remarkable for a town with less than 7,000 residents! Imagine the value and power of the combined hours donated in all the cities. Then consider the value of all the in-kind contributions: the hardware stores that donate paint, builders who offer construction help, newspapers that sponsor garden makeover contests, nurseries that help with civic plantings, people who grow plants for the town in their greenhouses or backyards.

Participation

Through 2014, more than 220 communities from 40 states have participated in our annual awards program; the lives of more than 22 million people have been touched in some way by America in Bloom. When you add to that the people in neighboring towns, our remarkable reach has touched the lives of millions more Americans.

About the Author

Marvin N. Miller is market research manager for Ball Horticultural Company, West Chicago, Illinois. Marvin has a B.S. in horticulture, a M.S. in Agricultural Economics from Purdue University and a Ph.D in Food and Resource Economics, majoring in Agricultural Marketing, from the University of Florida. He has been with Ball Horticultural Company since 1983. The focus of his research efforts involves the changing structure, conduct, and performance of the horticulture industry, with current emphasis on North American floriculture. He travels extensively, visiting greenhouses and retail establishments, and frequently writes and speaks about trends affecting the industry. Marvin is also active in a number of industry organizations and currently serves on boards for the Seeley Conference (Cornell University) and the American Floral Endowment. Marvin served as President of the Board of Directors of America in Bloom from 2005 until March, 2014. He also serves on committees for the Society of American Florists, AmericanHort, and other horticultural industry organizations and has served on several advisory committees for the U.S. Department of Agriculture and a number of universities.

About the Editor/Designer

The concept for this book was conceived by Evelyn Alemanni who has been an America in Bloom judge since 2003 and board member since 2008. She chairs the external relations committee and is the author of AIB's 'Best Ideas' book series (the rights to which she donated to AIB) and many other books. As a gift to America in Bloom, Evelyn compiled all of Dr. Miller's articles, designed the book, created print-ready files, and managed its publication.

Contents

Contents

Contents

I Talk to the Trees

March 2014

"I talk to the trees
But they don't listen to me
    I talk to the stars
But they never hear me
    The breeze hasn't time
To stop and hear what I say
I talk to them all in vain
    But suddenly my words
Reach someone else's ear
At someone else's heart strings too
    I tell you my dreams
And while you're listening to me
I suddenly see them come true."

These words, as sung by Clint Eastwood in the 1969 movie *Paint Your Wagon*, a remake of the Broadway musical of the same name by Alan Jay Lerner and Frederick Loewe, captured my thinking during a recent snow-shoeing trek in Alaska's Denali National Park. Yet, as I trudged through deep snow, I couldn't help but feel a connection to nature unlike the ones I experience during warmer times and with more assured footing. The quiet of winter, interrupted only by the crunching of snow beneath my marching feet, still offered the opportunity to reflect, in part due to the low angle of the sun in that northern latitude and the cold. The earth was blanketed with white. Evidence of man's presence was hidden. And it was beautiful!

As I hiked, I couldn't help but think about America in Bloom. I have often felt many of America's communities look particularly glorious when blanketed with snow. While winter isn't the season for most flowers (Hellebores being one beautiful exception in many parts of the country), snow does both an exquisite job of outlining trees and of covering man's sins. And the winter landscape, as alternately defined by a blanket of snow, offers new perspective and almost offers the landscaper the opportunity to begin anew.

Winter's solace also offers an opportunity for introspection. Thoughts of what might have been and of what yet may be often converge during quiet moments. A clean slate. Virgin footsteps. Winter quiet. New perspectives. Fresh ideas.

Over the years, I can't begin to guess how many people I personally have talked to about America in Bloom. I've talked about city beautification and community enhancement. I've talked about our judging criteria and a community's constituent groups. I've certainly talked about the impacts flowers, plants, trees, and shrubs can have on one's life and on a community's well-being, attributes that go way beyond being pretty through economic, environmental, psychological, and sociological avenues. Conversations aside, our monthly e-newsletter directly reaches nearly 15,000 folks, and I know many of the recipients forward the newsletter to others, sometimes including entire association memberships or city administrations. And my conversations and writings have only joined the chorus of other volunteers who have shared similar messages with many cities, with many volunteer groups, and with countless others who have similarly shared their passions about America in Bloom. And yet, in the quiet of a snow-filled landscape, there is reflection, and you can't help but wonder if anyone has heard the many stories that plants have to offer.

Then almost suddenly, while still in Alaska, I received word that registration has closed for the thirteenth season of our National Awards Program. I am gratified to learn that 33 cities will be involved this year, an 18% increase over last year and our highest program enrollment in 9 years. We have 11 new cities in the program this year and 22 returning communities, testifying both to value we have brought to cities in the past and to the new opportunities we have yet to deliver.

Suddenly the doubt is erased. There is evidence that the message has been heard. Folks ARE listening. Dreams ARE coming true.

Winter is a great season to plan, and with the official advent of Spring over the next few days, we can hope that Winter's solace and introspection will lead us all to knowing our dreams can come true.

"I tell you my dreams
And while you're listening to me
I suddenly see them come true."

"And You Shall Teach Them to Your Children"

February 2014

My first recollections of gardening were those of a first-grader. I distinctly remember helping my father plant and care for a row of tomato plants along the side of the house we rented. The plants were staked and tied with strips of old bed sheets. And as the plants got pollinated and tomatoes grew, I was there alongside my dad, helping to harvest the ripe, juicy fruits. Running that first big red tomato into the house to see my mother's reaction was also quite the experience. I could say, "We grew this!" as if we had handled the bees, watered, and fertilized the plants and watched the fruit size up and ripen with 24-hour surveillance.

As I grew older, the house and garden changed to a slightly larger property, and I took over the responsibility of much of the gardening activity. I learned that Mother Nature was in charge, and that the garden was just part of a larger environment that, along with me, equally affected our success. But I still consulted with my parents, as the garden was often part of dinner or other conversations. But if asked, even today, how I got into horticulture, I go back to those first-grade experiences under my father's tutelage. Though the biblical verse about teaching your children that "the Lord is One" is much more heady, I dare suggest that teaching your children to garden will have equally great rewards. Horticulture can certainly make for a great career! Yet, gardening can also provide for a life-long avocation, as well.

Recent market research, comparing gardeners to non-gardeners, has confirmed that gardeners are much more likely to have had parents who gardened. Indeed, in a recent study, 75 percent of gardeners reported their parents gardened, while only 58 percent of non-gardeners made the same claim about their parents. (I dare suggest than grandparents, too, can play a role, but this was not studied in this research.) Furthermore, gardeners reported helping their parents with the gardening activities, as children, 60 percent of the time; this compared with only 39 percent of non-gardeners, who said they, too, helped with gardening activities when young.

Finally, when gardeners were asked to classify themselves as enthusiastic versus casual gardeners, 73 percent of those who claimed to be enthusiastic gardeners reported viewing gardening as a family activity, while 43 percent of casual gardeners preferred to garden alone.

Clearly, people garden for various reasons. Casual gardeners reported gardening for mostly extrinsic reasons, claiming flowers and plants added beauty, improved curb appeal, and were a reflection of themselves. Enthusiastic gardeners were more likely to cite intrinsic values as their motivation, and claimed gardening reduced stress, was relaxing, connected them to nature, and expressed their creativity. Not surprisingly, enthusiastic gardeners tended to spend more time and more money on the gardening activities than did the casual gardeners.

Gardening can certainly provide rewards throughout one's lifetime. As with most good things in life, having the right nurturing start can make all the difference in the world. A good beginning can create the passion needed to make gardening an enriching endeavor throughout one's lifetime. Yet, I must ask if your city is doing all it can to portray gardening in a positive light? Is gardening part of the curriculum in your city's schools? Is your own garden a positive reflection on your gardening values and passion?

Why not plan now to plant some pride in your community this year? There's no telling what impact it might have on a first grader.

Another Look at Green Spaces

January 2014

For years, we've talked about the benefits of green spaces in urban environments. Indeed, our America in Bloom website contains several references to scientific studies which can be used to argue for more green spaces, whether we talk about the benefits of crime reduction, improved memory retention or students' test scores, stress reduction, increased creativity, quicker post-surgery recuperation, better neighborhood relations or the like.

Now, from Britain's European Centre for Environment and Human Health at the University of Exeter Medical School comes the report of a new study that adds tremendously to this knowledge base. Researchers examined data from over a thousand individuals. From this data they were able to characterize the benefits of moving to greener or less green neighborhoods within urban areas and how such moves affected mental health. The study used the General Health Questionnaire scores of individuals participating in the British Household Panel Survey.

Only scores from persons that could be tracked for five consecutive years, who had relocated during between 1991 and 2008, were considered. Researchers were able to conclude that individuals who moved to greener areas had significantly better and improving mental health in all three post-move years. In contrast, individuals who moved to less green neighborhoods showed significantly worse mental health in the year prior to the move, relative to their original baseline year, but these folks returned to their former baseline scores in the post-move years. However, those in this latter group never achieved the higher mental health scores of the group that moved to greener areas.

Mental health is indeed a critical public health issue. The World Health Organization has concluded that unipolar depressive disorders are now the leading cause of disability in medium to high income countries. With over three-fourths of the population in the world's more developed regions now living in urban areas, it is easy to accept the findings of a number of studies which have concluded that decreased access to "natural" spaces is affecting people's abilities to cope with stress. Similar conclusions have been found in a number of studies for a range of physical health outcomes, including mortality. However, this study, which documented sustained mental health improvements for those moving to greener urban areas, suggests that sustainable public health benefits can be achieved if environmental policies to increase urban green space are implemented.

At America in Bloom, our mission is to promote nationwide beautification through education and community involvement by encouraging the use of flowers, plants, trees, and other environmental and lifestyle enhancements. We envision communities across the country that as welcoming and vibrant places to live, work, and play – benefitting from colorful plants and trees; enjoying clean environments; celebrating heritage; and planting pride through volunteerism. Captured in these sentiments is the appreciation that greener communities are safer and healthier places for all their inhabitants. Now we have increased evidence that these communities also deliver better mental health, as well.

Very Lucky to Appreciate Plant Architecture
December 2013

Though my parents once shared with my undergraduate college advisor a photo of me wearing a straw hat, my first cognitive recollection of dealing with plants was when I was six years old. We grew some tomato plants on the side of the house we rented, and I remember tending these with my father throughout that summer. Staking, watering, weeding, tying, and harvesting were required that year, and the time spent provided me with my first insights into the structures of plants.

Over the years, I've had many other opportunities to admire plant structure up close. Certainly, in my early teens, when I read about pruning and was suddenly entrusted with the loppers and pruning saws, I got a great appreciation for a tree's branches, crotches, trunks, and bark. When the four American elms on the property died as a result of Dutch elm disease, I learned about shade and its sudden disappearance. Planting a replacement oak just before I went off to college, I got a great appreciation for siting, then digging a hole larger than the root ball, then filling, tamping, watering, and finally mulching the new garden resident after it was carefully situated into the hole. A year or two later, I remember noticing an acorn that had sprouted nearby, and I watched the race over the successive decades to see that Pin Oak seedling's height overtake that of the Willow Oak I had planted as a tree already three times my height.

As a horticulture major during my undergraduate years, I really learned a totally different way to appreciate plant structure. I learned about sexual and asexual plant propagation, about grafting, about xylem and phloem, and about the cambium layer lying in between. I learned to recognize many species, as woody ornamental identification was followed by Herbaceous I and Herbaceous II Plant Identification. Learning to sketch a plant's discernible qualities for later identification makes you really notice a plant's particular characteristics quite closely.

In graduate school, the sketching pencil was replaced by a camera, and a whole new way to appreciate plants was revealed. As I employed this new technology first for documentation and years later to photographically "capture" what was in my mind's eye, I gained many other perspectives on plants. These views were sometimes focused on the smallest of details, yet at other times, the attention was aimed at the grandest of angles. And with the camera, I could record an image, as well, which others could see.

Appreciating plants has been a lucky endeavor for me. The fact that I still can be amazed by both nature's strength and delicate fragility has kept me easily satisfied with the beauty she offers. And though we might think Mother Nature does a pretty terrific job on her own, at this time of year, we often see man's hand helping to accentuate the curves she makes and highlighting the structures she has created.

Man has often utilized nature's architecture as a guiding principle for our arts and our crafts. We talk of the family tree, and utilize a tree-like graphic to display subsequent generations all ascending from the same source. We follow nature's curves to help us design roads, tracks, and ship keels, and we employ nature's bounty to build our homes, our businesses, and our places of worship. We look to nature to help challenge our imagination, while at the same time reassuring our emotions. And throughout our existence, nature is there to inspire, to challenge, and to allow us to appreciate her beauty.

Advocate, Network, Lead, and Champion
November 2013

Along with two other America in Bloom (AIB) board members, I have just returned from the National League of Cities' annual Congress of Cities and Exposition. This event regularly draws mayors, city managers, and city council members from cities across America, all looking for best practices they might adopt or adapt for their cities. America in Bloom has been attending this event for about a decade trying to encourage more cities to embrace our program and to learn the power of horticulture to improve lives. Invariably, our booth has been the only exhibit that has shown off any horticulture with the intent of suggesting that flowers, trees, shrubs, turf, and groundcovers have a role to play in the urban environment for environmental, psychological and sociological, and even economic reasons.

While at the event this year, part of our AIB delegation attended a workshop titled "Shifting Expectations for Neighborhoods in Transition." Moderated by City Councilwoman Lavonta Williams of Wichita, Kansas, panelists included Mr. Scot Spencer, Associate Director for Advocacy and Influence at the Center for Community and Economic Opportunity of the Annie E. Casey Foundation; City Councilman Michael Wojcik from Rochester, Minnesota; and Mr. Ron Sims, former Deputy Secretary of the U.S. Department of Housing and Urban Development. Mr. Spencer spoke of the incredible work his foundation is undertaking in the City of Baltimore, Maryland, in revitalizing a part of East Baltimore where the average annual income is about 25 percent of the average for the state, even though this neighborhood sits in the shadows of the world-famous Johns Hopkins Hospital medical complex. Mr. Wojcik represents a district that includes the world-famous Mayo Clinic, yet it, too, contains neighborhoods which are in transition and filled with many vacancies – uninhabited homes, empty buildings, and vacant lots. And Secretary Sims spoke not only of his experiences at HUD earlier in the Obama Administration but also his time in the Seattle area serving on the city and county government during which he, too, dealt with many neighborhoods in transition.

Even though panel members spoke about the debt crisis from the recent recession and its lingering effects, about the need for public transportation to be accessible to those in neighborhoods, and about the need for revitalized urban neighborhoods to be attractive to those with multicultural, multi-ethnic, and multi-socio-economic backgrounds, the one thing all agreed on was the importance for updated landscaping to be part of the improved neighborhoods. Mr. Sims cited studies in proclaiming that green communities yielded 70 percent less crime and called flowers and plants unequivocally the best crime-fighters we can ever have!

Panelists insisted that making neighborhoods walkable was a key to reducing crime and ultimately a key to revitalizing neighborhoods. Mr. Sims noted there were no 90 degree corners in nature and that a neighborhood which can eliminate blind corners, perhaps, by using plants at street corners, will encourage people to walk. He argued that, in the best of all scenarios, a city ideally should have a park within one-quarter mile of every resident but called it essential that parks be within a half mile of all. If parks are farther from residents' homes, Sims insisted, people will not walk and this leads to inactivity and ultimately obesity. Sims also praised community gardens as being incredibly good, incredibly healthy, and incredibly safe places in the community.

During the question and answer period, the importance of green spaces was reinforced with Mr. Spencer noting that land needed to be set aside during the urban renewal process to incorporate green spaces, even if it meant sacrificing what was once property on the tax rolls. He talked about several new parks being incorporated into the East Baltimore neighborhoods being reinvigorated. Mr. Sims concurred with this assessment. While Mr. Wojcik suggested there could be other ways to incorporate green spaces by using pre-existing right-of-ways along streets and sidewalks, he, too, suggested creating walkable communities as a key to revitalizing our cities.

At AIB, we have testified to plants' ability to deter crime for many years. In fact, our AIB website (www.americainbloom.org) includes several links to articles that discuss the plant and crime-reduction phenomenon. And our "Discover the Surprising Side of Plants" brochure, downloadable from the AIB website, testifies to this benefit plus many others that plants provide. It is our belief that, just as the panelists at this workshop testified, it is important that people have both an active and a passive connection to plants – people need to be close to plants and people need to have plants close to them.

So, we encourage you to advocate for the importance of having plants in your community. We encourage you to network with others to help spread the word. Lead by example by encouraging your city to add green spaces. And be a champion for green spaces in your community.

America in Bloom certainly can help with this journey, and we would welcome your participation in our programs.

The Greater Economic Good
October 2013

The recent shutdown of the Federal government (thankfully now concluded), believe it or not, helped to reinforce several points we have often made in this e-newsletter, at least in my mind. We have frequently noted that plants are more than pretty. Indeed, city beautification efforts are good for the environment, good for the sociological and psychological well-being of the community's citizens, and also good for the economic vitality of the city.

On this last point, we have often noted that trees, flowers, shrubs, turf, and groundcovers can help to add to property values, and therefore, can help to increase a city's tax base. We have cited that when plants are used, they can attract shoppers to a shopping district, tenants to business parks and office buildings, guests to hotels, and renters to apartment complexes. And we have noted that visitors are often attracted to well-landscaped cities and towns, as people just enjoy being in beautiful surroundings.

During the recent shutdown, several states petitioned the Federal government to re-open closed National Parks, National Monuments, and National Recreation Areas with state, and sometimes, county and municipal funds. And while these locations sometimes involved natural wonders, in certain instances, it was the fact that autumn is often a critical time for visitors to infuse cash into the local economies.

On a personal note, I was traveling in New Hampshire's White Mountains during part of the shutdown. In the White Mountain National Forest, bathrooms, campgrounds and other facilities were closed, and the U.S. Forest Service had posted signs explaining the closures were related to the shutdown and that facilities would re-open once Congressional funding was restored. But since the Kancamagus Highway, which runs through the National Forest, is also New Hampshire's Route 112 connecting the cities of Bath, Easton, Woodstock, Albany, and Conway, there was a beautiful unrestricted passage through the woods. There was no doubt that these communities rely on the annual pilgrimage of tourists seeking to view fall color. And the number of tour buses I saw likely did not disappoint. Even as the tourists were inconvenienced by the closed facilities, they still came, and they emptied their wallets into the cash drawers of restaurants, hotels, and gift shops throughout the state.

This same sort of entourage descends upon countless cities and towns across America during many times of the year. I was once told by a prominent businessman in an AIB city, Vernal, Utah (population 9,089), that the 7-Eleven in town sold more disposable cameras (before digital cameras were part of every cell phone) than any other retailer in the state, a state which boasts five National Parks. These cameras largely were sold to folks passing through Vernal, who were amazed at all of the flowers planted along Vernal's main thoroughfares. In the process, visitors often made unplanned stops for meals and hotels, thereby pumping dollars into the local economy.

When Boeing was contemplating where to relocate from Seattle several years ago, the decision on where to move came down to two cities. Chicago's Mayor Daley asked the Chicago Park District to prepare something showcasing the beauty of Chicago's parks. The resulting video presentation helped propel the city into the winning position as Boeing's new corporate home.

And we know of a number of cities that have included municipal landscaping projects as a regular beneficiary of at least part of the city's take of hotel visitor taxes. Indeed, in countless locations around the country, plants help make the tourist experience memorable from the moment visitors disembark at airport terminals, along the boulevards to downtown business districts, and even along the way to convention centers and nearby hotels. In past conversations with convention and visitor bureau executives, we often have heard their perspectives that plants help to set their cities apart from other locations.

So, the next time you hear folks questioning landscaping budgets, at least give pause and consider the likely impact of the landscapes that are created. It could be that the pennies spent per citizen, per business, or per visitor might just be generating dollars that serve the greater economic good.

An Embarrassment of Riches

September 2013

The other day, I was talking to a garden center manager about America in Bloom. The manager knew of the program, but when I asked why they had not brought the program to the city, the manager replied, "I don't want to come across as self-serving." "Self-serving?" I asked. When he replied, "Well, it could help my sales," I countered, "And the lives of all your fellow citizens!"

Unfortunately, this is not the first time I've had this conversation. I am the first to admit that a thriving America in Bloom program in a city can be very good for a garden center's business. Indeed, we have anecdotal evidence from one grower with several garden centers of his own across two states. This grower has convinced several of the cities where his garden centers operate to participate in America in Bloom's Awards Program. While not all of the cities participate in the program every year, this grower has offered the comment that his garden centers' sales average sales were 8 percent higher in the years those cities participate than during the years the cities "take off." Still, because the cities have participated, even during the "off" years, his garden centers sell more today than they did prior to the initial involvement in the AIB program.

However, other businesses benefit, too! Cities with beautification efforts just make for nicer places to shop, so the involvement with America in Bloom helps most of the merchants in the towns. And pretty places also attract more visitors, so hotels and restaurants prosper as well. This kind of success often attracts new residents over time, which, in turn, again helps all of the merchants and maybe even some in the construction trade and others in the service industry.

A flourishing community helps the tax base for that municipality as well. This can ultimately lead to either a reduction in the tax rate and/or to an increase in the city's services. And so the cycle continues. Done right, the city will just get prettier and prettier over time. And this could lead to a host of other environmental, as well as sociological and psychological, benefits as well.

So, when I have one of these conversations with a garden center owner or manager, I always leave by challenging them to get even more involved with the community and get the community involved with America in Bloom. If challenged about being self-serving, the correct response is, "Yes! It will help my business. But it will help the businesses throughout this community. It will help all of the citizens as well. And it will help the city government. You're damn right, I'm self-serving, and I'm proud to be so!"

Thoughts About August

August 2013

I recently saw an article that bemoaned what the month of August has become and longed for that slower period, when August was a lazier time likened to the calm before the storm. The author noted that with school bells ringing earlier and earlier in the year, August's reputation as a quiet time had given way to a rather hectic period, filled with back-to-school preparations and the like. Indeed, the stereotypical reports of what one did during their summer vacations are now delivered in the classrooms during the time when those vacations once took place. The author compounded the contrast by noting that the everyday pace of life has quickened, and the idea that there should be a "down time," as August once was, was so foreign to many that we may never again experience true relaxation.

I found the article both disconcerting and yet comforting, for I knew exactly what the author meant, but I also recognized the antidote. Life's pace has indeed been altered. Cell phones, emails, and text messages all provide additional and faster ways to stay in touch. The traditional activities once associated with a post-Labor Day period, now get accomplished weeks earlier, so we can all "get a jump on things." Truth be known that when we all accelerate the pace, no one really gets a jump on anyone. It is just as if the starter's gun has fired that much earlier, and the race is on for all contestants.

Yet, life's respite is just a garden away. When I "go to the garden," I leave the world behind. When I get my daily dose of nature, my natural sense of balance is restored. A visit to a park allows one to recompose one's compass, to change direction, even for a moment, so that things are kept in perspective and the "natural order" is restored. The great thing about this attitude is this can be done in August or in any month and with great planning or just on the spur of the moment.

Chicago's former Mayor Daley had a unique perspective about parks in the urban environment. He wanted every citizen to be within a few blocks of a park, specifically so that nature's recuperative role was within easy reach. When city-owned vacant land for such parks was found scarce within certain neighborhoods, he looked to the Chicago Board of Education to transform the blacktop playgrounds that often surrounded classroom buildings into public parks that just happened to contain a school in their midst.

The experiment proved successful on so many fronts. First, the mayor got his parks. Secondly, the neighborhoods adopted these school grounds-turned-parks as their own, and the vandalism the school buildings experienced was dramatically reduced. The ranks of school advisory boards, which had often been depleted by lack of commitment, swelled for the first time in years. And the most amazing result was that grades of the students in the schools shot up, as students reportedly were more focused on school work after being exposed to green spaces during their recesses.

Ancillary benefits were also derived. Crime statistics dropped in many neighborhoods, perhaps as a result of more people being out and about. Property values also increased for homes in close proximity to the parks. And Chicagoans reported a "greater sense of place" in the proximities nearest the parks, perhaps, because the parks provided reference points with which whole neighborhoods could relate and occasionally gather.

Parks certainly can become great places for those seeking a respite from the normal hectic pace of life. Yet, many of the benefits associated with public parks can also accrue to those who create a park-like setting in their own surroundings. I know a visit to my yard provides a great start and/or end to my day, and I have heard from countless neighbors who tell me their daily constitutional often includes travel to my block, specifically to see what is in bloom in my yard. Park-like settings at businesses and office parks can also create oases for guests and employees to gather and relax.

While exposure to things natural won't replace those lazy, hazy days of Augusts gone by, it is nice to know that even in the hectic-paced lives we now lead, that nature can still deliver a breather when a deep breath alone is not quite enough.

These are Trees I Remember Playing Under in My Youth
July 2013

Last month, I wrote about the value of trees. I cited many of the benefits we often discuss: the ability of trees to reduce smog, to reverse the effects of climate change, to improve mental health, to produce oxygen while sequestering carbon, and the like. But in just this past week, my perspective of a tree's value was broadened, as I traveled with a pair of America in Bloom judges, shadowing them, as they evaluated the city where I've worked for almost 30 years, West Chicago, Illinois.

Over the 12 years of America in Bloom, I have spoken with many judges, attended judges training several times, read more than a few judges' evaluations, and counseled both judges and city volunteers about their judging experiences. I have also interacted with judges while they were judging several nearby communities. I feel I have had a good perspective of what the judges go through. I also have a new-found perspective on what the cities go through while preparing for judges' visits, while hosting the judges and touring them through their communities, as well as the aftermath, when judges counsel cities on what they were both positively and not-so-positively impressed with. But this is the first time I have spent two full days with our pair of judges as they completed their visits to a community, and I was not prepared for one particular emotional experience.

This week's travel indeed did provide a new impression for me, when I heard the park district's contract forester, Phil Graf, tell the story of cleaning up downed trees following a massive storm of a year ago that hit West Chicago's Reed-Keppler Park. The July 1, 2012 storm destroyed and damaged trees in the city's largest park (118 acres) in the center of town. In total, the park lost 163 trees, including 81 mature red, white, and burr oaks. Overall, 15.6 percent of the park's tree canopy was destroyed in a matter of moments. But what made the telling so emotional was the line Forester Graf used as he described, for probably the hundredth time in the last year, the utter devastation that greeted him following the storm: "These are trees I remember playing under in my youth."

In that one line, I acknowledged professionalism and dedication. I recognized a sense of community and heritage. I certainly experienced both his emotion as well as my own. But I also discovered a new significance to associate with trees: Memories. His story reflected his childhood memories, as well as those of countless others who had visited Reed-Keppler Park. His emotion recalled my childhood memories from hundreds of miles away, just as they recalled his, just minutes from where we were meeting. His line reflected the community's heritage and explained his professionalism and his dedication.

The memory created by a tree: this was indeed a new and meaningful experience!

Volunteerism, Transformation, and Rejuvenation
May 2013

I often get asked why a city should enter the America in Bloom program. It is as if the questioner is asking what the payback will be for the city. And while cities differ in their approaches, I often think of a few key words in my responses.

Certainly, volunteerism has to be at the top of the list. In community after community, we are told that our America in Bloom program really has inspired citizens to turn out, to roll up their sleeves, and to contribute countless hours for the public good. In some cities, this has evolved into a standing volunteer corps that can be called upon to help in many different venues for many different activities, even beyond those involving the America in Bloom efforts. Volunteer efforts often involve youth, as schools sometimes challenge students, and youth groups frequently challenge members, to contribute a certain minimum number of hours toward community improvement efforts. And the youth often inspire adults to volunteer as well. Recorded efforts include not only the planting and maintenance of flowers and plants, but the building and restoration of entire parks, the collection of litter, the painting of decaying structures, and the like. In some communities, youth groups have helped to close generation gaps, as they have turned into senior citizen volunteer corps to help the elderly with garden and home maintenance issues.

Transformation also occurs. Sometimes the recommendations which our judges provide offer enough impetus to alter the attitudes and the fortunes of citizens and cities alike. It is amazing, but the power of the outside visitors' comments often provides the stimulus needed, and America in Bloom is proud to say we have often been a meaningful change-agent in this regard. We can site examples where suggestions have led to buildings being demolished and/or rebuilt, remodeled, or rehabilitated to provide housing for new residents and visitors. An armory turned into a theater, a train station transformed into an art gallery, warehouses turned into condominiums, riverfronts turned into historic educational trails, and vacant lands or abandoned lots turned into parks are just some of the examples of the transformative power of America in Bloom judges' recommendations in action.

A big benefit for many cities from America in Bloom involvement has to be rejuvenation. Cities that plant trees, flowers, shrubs, turf, and other groundcovers really can change the whole perspective of townspeople and visitors alike. The city literally looks to have rolled out the welcome mat. Visitors immediately notice the vibrancy radiating from the city, its businesses, and its residents. Tourism increases. The tax base improves due to increased sales tax revenues. People socialize more. Crime is reduced. Spirits improve as other psychological and sociological benefits of greening accrue. Students remember more and do better in school when exposed to green spaces. People are generally happier. Businesses and residents invest more in the community, as they aspire to even loftier visions of what the city could become.

Certainly, when adopted by a city, America in Bloom can become truly inspirational. While we have often seen results from a single AIB interaction, we have seen tremendous growth when a city has institutionalized the America in Bloom program over time with a sustained effort. This is when America in Bloom really shines. Cities have seen measurable improvements in property values as green spaces are developed, as properties are rehabilitated, and as citizens unify for the common good. Economic development results, as businesses are attracted, as residential turnover stabilizes, as wages rise, and as the average citizen truly bonds with his city. This is when pride becomes entrenched and residents call a city home.

At America in Bloom, we often talk about pride. We even say we're all about "planting pride in our communities." We certainly welcome your support!

Down with Silos

April 2013

I have just returned from a long week traveling the California coast from San Diego to San Francisco, looking at the new things breeders are preparing for introduction to the gardening trade over the next year or so. This event, which the horticultural trade refers to as "Spring Trials," is a tradition that began about 40 years ago by one breeder. Within 10 years it grew into an industry-wide event. Originally, the event provided distributors and their sales forces the opportunity to see what was coming down the pike for introduction from breeders for the following spring. About 15 years ago, the event also began attracting the largest growers, who wanted to see the new introductions for themselves. Soon after, buyers for the largest national chains and even for many regional chains also began to attend. And in the spirit of true cooperation, all of the industry's breeders picked the same week to showcase their wares for all to see.

Historically, the event was known as "Pack Trials," because most of the breeding showcased seed annuals and the various companies would trial their new varieties against the market leaders of the same species, using bedding plant packs sown at the same time, as the consistent factor across the trial. Over time, more and more new breeding included vegetatively-propagated materials, and some switched to larger pots or even large planters in which to trial their new releases. Slowly, the term "pack" was replaced with "spring" to be more inclusive. Also, more recently, perennials and shrubs have infiltrated the week's offerings, and the propagative materials now include not only seeds and cuttings but also tissue-cultured liners, bulbs, roots, and more. The whole event has become more of a marketing opportunity for each company, and with few exceptions, little competitive trialing is shown.

Believe it or not, one of the drivers of these changes has been the consumer and her garden. At some point over the last decade or so, it became apparent to a number of the participating companies that the consumer wanted more for her garden than just the latest marigold, petunia, or pansy. Instead, her focus switched to beauty, and she really didn't care in which silo the industry wanted to put its creations. The consumer let it be known she was more concerned with garden performance, with disease and insect resistance, with drought tolerance, and with color than whether she was buying annuals or perennials, and she was certainly not concerned with how the plants were propagated. She was open to trying many new things, as long as they delivered on the aforementioned qualities. These traits transcended the industry silos, and the consumer voted with her pocketbook that these traits mattered most!

While she was voting, the consumer has also let it be known that she was interested in a few more issues. She is interested in shopping across retailers, recognizing that she might get better pricing at some places for the basics, but more unique offerings and information on how to grow these plants at others. The consumer has also argued for her concerns about the environment and her time, as well as other matters relating to the costs vs. benefits of the whole gardening enterprise. So the industry is now on notice that the plants it breeds have to be more than just pretty and that they must contribute to the greater good by being easier to produce and care for, by requiring fewer inputs in the way of time, water, and effort.

When possible, these plants also have to perform some heroic activities by making this world a better place. Plants are often called upon to contribute to environmental, economic, and psychological and sociological well-being, all while sequestering carbon, using carbon dioxide, and returning more oxygen to the atmosphere. Plants must indeed be miracle workers!

Breeders have certainly been busy trying to satisfy all of these demands, and the plants they've bred have come a long way. Marketers now are beginning to change how plants are sold, and the silos of old are slowly beginning to crumble. Perhaps, plants can serve as an example for others, both inside and outside of the garden, that silos may have a place and a time, but then again they may not, if the greater good is better served without them.

A New Beginning
March 2013

We often recognize spring as offering the opportunity for a new beginning. The season appears on the calendar in the Northern Hemisphere with a start of March 20, the day that the sun crosses the equator on its northward march. Day and night are about equal that day. Spring is also when the swallows return to San Juan Capistrano, California, though this actually happens the day before on March 19, St. Joseph's Day.

Spring also often denotes renewal. Many religions use this season to announce a new beginning. Symbolism includes eggs, chicks (are they spring chickens?), lambs, green grass, and flowers. In many cultures, spring is considered the "head of the year," and for some it is "the beginning of time" – perhaps, because many young animals are born in the spring. Spring is when fall-planted bulbs bloom, as they reach their crescendo after a long winter's nap. And spring is when redbuds, cherries, apples, and pears shout out their presence with blooms first, followed by new, lush, green leaves.

Spring is also a time when many businesses offer their new products – their "spring lines" – though sometimes their spring lines are actually working a year ahead. We see this in automobiles, furniture, fabrics, and clothing. We also see this in horticulture. Time is required for advanced planning, as it may take a full year to generate adequate production volumes and for marketing efforts to culminate with orders for products to appear at retail.

Arbor Day occurs in the spring of the year as well. Take time to plant that new tree! It may look small now, but in 20 or 30 years its bounty of shade, blossoms and/or fruit will reward you and/or the generation that follows with the knowledge that your foresight has paid off. Spring can also be a good time to assess where you are in life. Any signs of spring fever? Perhaps, it's time for the annual checkup with the doctor. If statistics are accurate, there's a good chance the doctor will tell you, "You need more exercise!" That's a great excuse to get out and about to breathe in that fresh spring air. Are the home and garden in good shape, or is a little spring cleaning needed? Maybe the car needs a spring tune-up. Many things may need to be assessed to be sure your house and belongings are in good order. Spring is also a great time to stop and smell the roses. In my part of the country, they may not bloom until June. When it happens, there will often be a line of folks waiting to catch a whiff. For America in Bloom cities, spring is also a time for preparation. Cities are finalizing their project plans in anticipation of the visit of the judges in the months to come. Work parties are cleaning up winter's debris – planting flowers, pruning and raking. Teamwork brings out the best in people. And whether it is realized at the time or not until sometime later, spring is also when the seeds of pride are planted for later harvest. Spring is a glorious time indeed. There is often a spring in our steps, and an attitude to behold. I love spring!

A Can-Do Attitude

February 2013

I recently attended a conference and enjoyed one of the speakers enough to ask for a copy of his presentation. As such, my request not only returned a link to his talk, but I now also have been added to his e-newsletter list and have begun receiving a stream of consciousness from him several times each week. This certainly is not what I hoped for, but so far, it has been a positive experience.

His most recent piece included an observation debating the difference between the saying, "Have a good day," which he argued was passive, and the remark, "Make it a good day." The latter is much more active, he contended, suggesting that a person has within their control the ability to have a good day, but only if they actively work at making it so. Within a few hours of receiving this e-newsletter, another arrived informing me that athletic apparel maker Under Armor was preparing to launch a new marketing campaign around the saying, "I will." I immediately compared this to Nike's "Just do it!" Both are active rather than passive lines, something quite fitting for athletic apparel, perhaps, but also quite in-concert with a "can-do attitude."

The arrival of these emails, almost simultaneously, may foretell a new can-do attitude sweeping this country. Certainly, the economic signs are pointing in positive directions, which may help to foster not only further economic recovery but more examples of can-do marketing slogans and more active approaches to life in general. I think we'll all welcome this positive approach.

Such vibrations fit well in a community setting that also includes an America in Bloom program. Our organization is all about bringing out the best in a city and helping to transform its citizens into an active volunteer force where folks take on vital roles in helping to shape a city's future. Certainly, a can-do attitude helps motivate volunteerism in the first place. Seeing the results from citizens pitching in to help make their city or town a better place to live is undeniably very rewarding. But witnessing people working, with identifiable results in their wakes, also has the tendency to attract others to join in the activities.

Volunteer efforts do coalesce around an identifiable cause. When a civic group pitches in for a cause, others tend to follow. In many AIB cities, if a Kiwanis, Rotary, or Lions Club gets involved, word soon spreads and other organizations' chapters decide to get "on board." If the Boy

Scouts join the parade, the Girl Scouts soon follow, as do the Cub Scouts, the Brownies, the Explorers, and other youth groups. If one hotel beautifies its property, others do so as well, if only for competitive reasons. If a business park on the east side of town updates its landscape, then the business park on the west side tends to follow suit. Similar results occur with condominium associations, churches, mosques and synagogues, shopping districts, and even private businesses. The Convention and Visitors Bureau involvement might begat participation from the Chamber of Commerce. The Historical Society's goal may become that of the city council. Elementary schools may spur on middle schools and high schools. The list of potential participants is almost endless.

In similar fashion, communities often have benefited from this "keeping up with the Joneses" effect. When neighbors spruce up their lots, whether it's from painting their homes, improving the landscape, or even just picking up litter, it often results in other neighbors repeating the steps, thereby improving the whole neighborhood. And when neighborhoods get together for the sake of improvement, that, too, gets replicated and entire cities move forward.

What makes this phenomenon a reality? Leaders with can-do attitudes – people who make it a good day. These individuals are almost always focused on the mission and seldom on themselves. These individuals are not afraid to roll up their sleeves and do the work alongside other volunteers. They lead by example, but they also keep the mission at the center of attention. The mission is identified, verbalized, and praise is extolled for each incremental step towards the ultimate goal. It's all about what we can do together! The end result is a win – a win for all involved, including all of the citizens of the city or town. The city not only looks prettier, but it acts prettier as well. Indeed, it might just be brimming with pride. That's why our byline reads: "America in Bloom: Planting Pride in Our Communities!"

A Blank Slate

January 2013

Last week I had the chance to visit a brand new garden center. It was so new that there were absolutely no plants in the greenhouse or nursery but only a few near the entrance to welcome visitors to the open house. The opportunity reminded me of what many gardeners – at least those in parts of the country that get freezing temperatures – might be viewing in mid-winter as they look at their gardens from the indoor-comfort of their homes. It's a blank slate, waiting for spring.

At the same time, I know the avid gardeners among us are probably scouring the pages of their mail-order gardening catalogs looking for inspiration for the coming season. This is what gardeners do in the dead of winter. Mail-order garden companies know that. That's why our mailboxes are filled to capacity this time of year. They call it inspiration. (The post office calls it revenue.)

For many gardeners (if not most), spring will involve several trips to the garden retailers in the area. (The average gardener visits over three retailers for their gardening needs each spring.) The trips are made to collect the plants that will transform that now-blank slate into a statement for the gardener and his or her visitors. The statement also shouts to passersby that, "A gardener lives here." And the individual statements of various homeowners collectively say something about a neighborhood, and neighborhoods collectively say something about a city or town. The messages are plenty and well-known: beauty, care, and pride.

Make no mistake, a community effort to plant or even to coordinate individual plantings is great. It is, after all, the basis of the many programs for cities involved in America in Bloom. Yet a recent study conducted at the University of Illinois to document the proliferation of community gardens found that, in the Chicago area, almost 75 percent of the total garden area was in home gardens, even in the urban environment and even in this city which prides itself for its public plantings. (Chicago is one of our America in Bloom cities!)

So, what gets planted in the garden? It often is a reflection of results (what was planted in the past that worked), relationships (what a friend or relative has planted), or other recommendations. These three R's say a lot about many of the gardens in this country. The other big influence is impulse – what looks good at the point of sale. Incorporated into these influences, of course, is habit. We all have a habit of using the same few species over and over again. It's easy to do once we find a reliable player that deals with our soil, our climate, our water and our level of care.

"Old reliables" tend to dominate our landscapes. The planting of "old reliables" is most common among annuals. Yet, we can see the pattern also used in perennials, trees and shrubs, especially in homeowner associations, residential developments, and other instances where one person or firm influenced an entire landscape.

Unfortunately, in parts of the United States, the planting of "old reliables" en masse is coming into question. Sometimes this occurs because a certain plant was widely used before its long-term characteristics were revealed. The Bradford Pear, an ornamental tree valued for its shape, its beautiful spring flowering, and even for its colorful fall leaves, provides an example. This tree was widely planted both as a street tree and in people's yards throughout a good part of the Eastern United States. Only after thousands were planted did folks come to realize that the tree often became quite brittle after it was 20 years old and ultimately a maintenance challenge.

Ash trees, prized for their many positive characteristics especially as shade trees, is an example of a tree that has fallen into disfavor in recent years because of Emerald Ash Borer, which is denuding neighborhoods in many states where ash trees were widely planted. This unfortunately follows the pattern of decline witnessed when American Elms succumbed to Dutch Elm Disease. (Elsewhere in this issue is an article relating the health of trees to human health, which suggests that wholesale decline of tree numbers in an area can lead to increased mortality related to cardiovascular and lower-respiratory-tract illnesses.)

Another "old reliable," but in the annuals category, is the common impatiens, Impatiens walleriana. Again, due to disease in parts of the country, the plant isn't quite that reliable anymore. Impatiens Downy Mildew (IDM) is a disease has been documented in the U.S. for over 100 years, but it has gone largely unnoticed until the last two gardening seasons. Even now, IDM appears to be a major threat only along the eastern seaboard, the upper Great Lakes, and in a few pockets on the West Coast, though this area is spreading. Where it has raised its ugly head, planting the common impatiens has become a risky venture. (New Guinea impatiens are largely unaffected.) So, what's a gardener to do when the plant which has become habitually planted is no longer reliable? Simply put: begin anew. Seek advice from friends, neighbors, and other avid gardeners. In many communities, a master gardeners' program could be an excellent source of information. And if you have good garden retailers upon whom you can rely for solid advice, they too can serve as a source of information.

If you live in one of our America in Bloom cities, ask some of those involved what works for them. One of the great positives that has been reported by AIB cities is the great exchange of information that occurs not only between municipal, business and residential groups, but also the exchange of gardening information among all of those involved. Also, as the University of Illinois study suggested, don't be afraid to look over the backyard fence of a friend or neighbor for some inspiration and to see what's working for others.

Certainly as you stare at your blank slate, imagine the possibilities. The palette of choices is quite large. And there is a whole world of horticulture waiting to deliver once spring arrives.

Are They Real?

December 2012

Last month, AIB Board members Katy Moss Warner, Doug Cole, and I manned a booth in the Boston Convention Center to tout the message that floral displays, urban forestry, landscaped areas, environmental efforts, heritage preservation, and overall impression were important to cities and towns across America.

Thanks to plant contributions from Nunan Florist and Greenhouses, Olson's Greenhouses, Patrick Lyons Greenhouses, and D.S. Cole Growers, the America in Bloom booth at the National League of Cities' annual Congress of Cities Exposition was reportedly the prettiest in the show. It certainly was the only booth touting the importance of horticulture to a city's economic prosperity, and the only booth bragging about the ability of plants to improve the environmental conditions in and around a city. Our booth was also the only space that presented information about the ability of plants to improve the sociological and psychological well-being of the citizens within a community.

We were also the only booth that had flowers as the focus of the booth. Our primulas were strategically placed on our table at waist level, so passersby could look down upon their bright colors. Our mums were on the corner on the floor, so their bright colors would catch the wandering eyes at the intersection of the aisles. The cyclamen and the Christmas cactus were intermixed at the back of the booth, both high and low, to provide depth and to invite folks in. A few Christmas cactus were also perched atop the literature rack to attract attention and soften the hard edges of the hardware.

And the plants worked! They worked in much the same way they might work in a community. The plants attracted attention, in much the same way they might draw tourists to a community or shoppers to a business district. Plants helped slow the trade show traffic, in much the same way that plants can be used to slow automobile traffic in a city's thoroughfare. They brightened the moods of the mayors, the city managers, and the city councilmen, and public works directors walked the aisles, as attested to by the many comments from our visitors, just like plants do in any community nationwide.

The plants also challenged the senses. Visitor after visitor stopped to touch the plants. Some bent over to smell a plant or two. And a few even picked up a pot to capture the essence of the fragrance that might be there. Many questioned what the varieties were. A number asked where they might find them and seemed astonished to learn they were all New England grown within a 75-minute drive of the convention center.

But the most often asked question was, "Are they real?" Our insistence that they were seemed to challenge the sensibilities of the questioners repeatedly, as on numerous occasions the passersby stopped to closely examine the pots to be assured that there was potting mix that was "in use," holding the plants in the pots, providing moisture and, perhaps, some nutrition. Even Tim, the retired fireman of 32 years manning the National Fire Protection Association booth next to ours got into the act, testifying in his beautiful Boston accent that indeed the plants were real and that he knew the grower.

Ladies and gentlemen: These plants served their role in our trade show booth by helping to attract our target audience, those that might help us enroll a city in the America in Bloom national awards program. But these plants also underscored the need to have plants in a city. When even the civic leaders attending this show have to stop to examine plants closely and have to be assured repeatedly that they are real, even when they are convinced to the contrary, it serves as a clarion call that we have become too detached from nature! It challenges us that we need to do more, as a society, to reconnect people to plants and plants to people! It means we must do everything possible to spread the message that people need to be connected to plants in both active and passive ways, that people must consciously seek ways to connect with nature and that nature must be allowed to surround us in all we do.

It is my hope that you embrace the message that plants can offer much to make this earth and your community a better place for you and yours. I hope you will seriously consider what an America in Bloom program might do for your community and that you begin the New Year with a renewed commitment to enter and win a place in your hearts for America in Bloom.

Thanks to Our Donors
November 2012

As we come to a close of another calendar year and we consider the accomplishments of American in Bloom during 2012, it is important to remember that all of the benefits of AIB are made possible by the generous support of our AIB donors. They are the ones who make it possible in every respect. While each sponsor may have their own unique reason(s) for participating, one common realization is that America in Bloom is not just a beautification program. It is a QUALITY OF LIFE program that illustrates the value and relevancy of our industries products and services that is lacking so much today. I think they realize that AIB offers many economic benefits, as well as the benefits that go along with increased community involvement, bringing residents together on common goals, increased civic pride and true community spirit that results when everyone pitches in, decreased vandalism and crime, and the numerous environmental (eco-systems services) and health and well-being benefits that go along with being surrounded by flowers, shrubs, and trees in our municipal and residential environments. So THANK YOU to all our generous sponsors for making the ideals of America in Bloom come alive!

If the Opposite Was the True Goal

November 2012

Last month, I had the pleasure of representing America in Bloom at the Communities in Bloom (CiB) Symposium in Edmonton, Alberta, Canada. During the symposium, I was awestruck by the message of one keynote speaker who, during his speech, employed a tactic from his high school teaching days. Frustrated with the attitudes of a group of teenagers, he asked his students to consider how they would go about preparing for life if their goal was not how to succeed in their careers, but how to fail. Steps such as skipping class, failing to study, doing drugs, and showing up drunk were among the obvious answers. Having written the suggestions on the board, he then engaged the students by asking them to contemplate the steps if the opposite was the true goal. "Instead," he asked, "how would you approach life if your goal was to succeed?"

In a similar fashion, Doug Griffiths, now Alberta's Minister of Municipal Affairs, asked the CiB symposium audience to consider their beautification objectives from a 180 degree perspective. He asked them to consider how they would proceed if the objective was to avoid beautification efforts, but instead had as their goal the challenge of embracing urban decay. Instead of planting flowers, trees, shrubs, and groundcovers, he asked, "How would you proceed if your goal was to convince folks to avoid planting these horticultural niceties? How would you proceed if the goal was to allow paint to chip, graffiti to overtake buildings, and litter to accumulate in the streets?" Indeed, he continued, "How would you proceed if you wanted to kill any sense of civic pride in your community?"

Griffiths suggested it might be a tough sale to convince folks to let property values slide and to lose all sense of pride in home and community. "Who among us would readily let decay overtake our community?" he asked. He begged, "Consider the consequences of such an approach."

A good way to kill civic pride would be to introduce divisiveness. A good way to eliminate the planting of plants would be to tax them excessively, to legislate against them, or to establish roadblocks that prevented folks from gathering together to improve their communities. A good way to initiate decline would be to remove all waste receptacles, reduce or eliminate garbage pick-ups, and the like. Politics aside, the discussion was such that it begged audience members to consider plants as pure luxuries that could not be afforded. If, on the other hand, beautification and civic pride were the true objectives, an all-out campaign to recruit volunteers to work towards the common goal would be warranted. It would be appropriate to organize the citizenry, to contemplate the rewards from working together, and to imagine how great each community could become. If progress is the true goal, it would be more important for everyone to pitch in to accomplish that goal even at the expense of worrying who got the credit for the efforts. And to add value to the concept, it is probably important to consider plants as necessities that no community could live without, if not for the beauty they bring, then for all of the added economic, psychological and sociological, and environmental benefits they bring to a community.

Indeed, the steps to embracing civic pride become more obvious if one, for a brief moment, considers what the opposite approach might be. As Thanksgiving approaches, let's be thankful that plants do indeed provide such a multitude of benefits for all to embrace.

Autumn Splendor

October 2012

Fall is my favorite time of the year. Being an avid gardener, bicyclist, and nature photographer, I like being outdoors year-round. (As a sign in a bicycle shop I frequent says, "There is no such thing as bad weather, just inappropriate clothing.") But autumn is a special time of the year, as it is when nature puts on her grand show.

I am lucky when it comes to fall. Not far from where I live is the Morton Arboretum, in Lisle, Illinois. The tree collection at the arboretum is quite grand, and the colors that nature displays are not to be missed. Each fall I find myself driving the arboretum's various loops repeatedly, with my windows down and sunroof open, drinking in as much of the autumn splendor as nature will allow. I might do some hiking, too, if time allows, but I can be quite content just breathing in the crisp autumn air. I always look forward to visiting the arboretum, but I especially look forward to my fall visits.

I am not alone. October is the arboretum's busiest month of the year. It gets so crowded that one might assume a burlesque show is being performed and people are lining up to see the performer's physique in the buff. Ironically, that's not too far off the mark. When nature drops her chlorophyll clothing to reveal the other pigments that have been hiding in the leaves all along, the anthocyanins and carotenoids take over unabashed. It is as if an orchestra has begun to play the concerto it has been practicing for the past year.

If you are fortunate enough to live as close to an arboretum as I, you know of the splendor to which I refer. But if you are close to a national forest or park, these, too, may provide an autumnal respite. I encourage all to get out and enjoy nature at her fullest glory. Check with local garden centers or farm markets to see if they are sponsoring events for family fun, as many will include corn mazes, hayrides, spook houses, and more in their fall lineups.

Autumn is also a great time to invest in a little fall color of your own. Fall is perfectly suited for planting most trees or shrubs. If you see a tree which has the color you favor, try taking a leaf to a local garden center and matching it to a plant you can call your very own. While there, consider picking up some garden mums or even some cabbage and kale, for these, too, provide the tremendous value of immediate color. And for a really great investment, in most parts of the country you can plant pansies or violas, which will provide color not only this fall but throughout the winter and into next spring. I know my recently planted pansies are already looking quite gorgeous. Enjoy the autumn and all that nature has to offer!

Doing Our Duty
September 2012

As most of you know, America in Bloom is a 501(c)(3) non-profit organization. As such, the organization cannot have any real opinions of its own. Yet, it is obvious to those that know us, that our organization does promote environmental awareness (one of our judging criteria), and we like to encourage the plantings of trees, shrubs, turf grass, and other groundcovers, as well as flowers. These pro-environmental leanings could label us in some circles, as having a certain political bias. Yet, it is the efforts that the citizens of our cities undertake when they enter our recognition program (working towards that common beautification goal), that makes them a united community. That, by itself, leans neither to the right nor the left.

Contrast this, for a moment, with the environment in Washington, D.C., as of late. Many pundits have noted the current environment in Washington is less than cordial. I personally feel it is the worst working environment I have seen in the more than 25 years of treks I have made to the Hill. You see, one of the things I get to do in my real "work-life" each year, whether I want to or not, is to go to Washington, D.C. I sometimes visit with folks at the U.S. Department of Agriculture and its various agencies, and I annually visit with the Illinois delegation of Senators and Representatives and their staffs. In my non-AIB work-life, I am active with the government relations programs of three industry organizations. (Incidentally, these organizations have been regular AIB contributors.) I currently serve on the government relations committees of two of these organizations and have served on another in the past. I guess being an industry statistician makes me popular when folks want to press a point about the industry's size and importance. Politicians who have co-sponsored certain bills in the past tell me there is no way they could even consider sponsoring the same bill today in the current Congress. I often wonder how the peer pressure from party leaders can be stronger than the pressure from constituents back home. And I wonder if it's their spine or their ego that is the most fragile body part. Leaders need strong spines, even if it costs them popularity points! Constituents need even stronger spines to reign in wayward politicians and to make sure their opinions are heard and acted upon.

Even in my AIB life, I often interact with politicians. Most of the municipal leaders we see in our America in Bloom cities are elected officials. (I know many of the readers of our e-newsletter are among this group.) These mayors and city councilmen generally have their ears-to-the-ground when it comes to local situations. They are the ones who tell us how rewarding it was to be involved with America in Bloom and what it has done for their cities by building "true community." I often see these municipal leaders when I help staff the AIB booth at the National League of Cities' Congress of Cities Exposition each fall. I look forward to meeting some of these mayors at our Symposium, later this week. And we even have a former mayor and a sitting mayor on the current AIB Board of Directors.

An issue that many speakers bring up at the National League of Cities meetings is the feeling of a disconnect between what goes on in Washington and what happens on Main Street U.S.A. I am sure many Americans feel this disconnect as well between what folks feel and how they perceive Washington is or isn't reacting to their real needs. Certainly, many of the protests across America in the last year have been based on the notion that politicians need to understand the real needs people have, and "wake up to this reality."

These concerns arise not only because it is the election season. While I am not naïve enough to expect every "promise" made on the campaign trail to be fulfilled, I do like to consider whether my elected representatives made good faith efforts to get things done and whether those efforts really align with my personal thinking. Coincidentally, a powerful motive I have is for politicians to work together with other legislators to get things done. (This reminds me of citizens working together for America in Bloom!) When efforts more often are in conflict, the politicians usually do not get my vote.

I try to get to know my elected officials. I tend to have a feeling of where they stand on the issues of importance to me. When I do not know where a candidate stands, I do the research, which may include a web search or writing the candidate for an opinion. I believe my duty is not only to cast a vote on Election Day, but also to know for whom and for what I am voting. Even if it wasn't almost time to go to the polls, it is always time to continue my efforts to know where the candidates stand and to try to persuade them to support my views on the issues.

During a recent visit, I was told by a representative that we would not discuss a certain issue. While the politician certainly does not have to agree with my views on a certain topic, to not even listen to where a constituent is coming from, suggests to me that this politician really cannot be representing me. Ultimately, this is a quick route to not getting my support.

So, my plea to those who don't like the current political situation is to do a little research. Consider contacting a representative to find out exactly where he or she stands. Consider the opponent as well. Determine who might be more likely to support your interests. And then please remember to vote on Election Day! Even if the politicians don't always match our thinking on every issue, at least in theory, they do represent us. And if they fail to do so, it is time to elect alternatives. Oh, and remember the environment as well!

Garden Matters

August 2012

I live in a neighborhood with a lot of walkers. We have folks who walk alone, as couples, and as small groups. Some walk with their four-legged companions, while others walk unencumbered. I've gotten to know many of these folks by sight. With others, a brief chat might begin and end with an exchange of pleasantries. For a few, I have longer conversations.

As I go about my garden tasks, I have gotten to know some of these neighbors quite well. Because I do much of my garden work early in the morning before work, I get to know the early-risers better than those I might see if I spent more time in the garden later in the day.

While gardening, I also am regularly visited by wildlife. My two birdbaths each seem to attract different birds and for different reasons. I get a lot of sippers at one, where the birds perch on the rim and take a drink; birds visiting here are in and out in a few seconds, and the turnover is quick. The other bird bath seems to attract the bathers, as most birds actually jump in and splash for several minutes at a time. If birds used washcloths, I am sure this second birdbath would have a towel rack filled with soiled rags, as the birds seem to aggressively wash under their wings, between their legs, and even behind their ears in this receptacle, and fresh water turns rather muddy in just a day.

I also have assorted chipmunks, squirrels, rabbits, butterflies, and bees visiting on a regular basis. The chipmunks like to run between the downspouts, hiding in the ends when I walk by. The squirrels are mostly about finding fallen nuts from neighboring black walnut or oak trees. And the rabbits seem to sit in the yard and say to one another, "Oh, look, there's a gardener," when I walk into the yard. I am sure more than a few flowers have provided food for this menagerie. The butterflies and bees also get food here, but they pollinate in the process.

Each summer, as August approaches and the flowers really start to come into their own, it seems my garden also attracts another breed. These are neighbors who apparently have been viewing my garden from a distance, either through windows from nearby homes or as they have driven by. They make a point of stopping when they see me in the yard, and asking about a certain flower or plant that has caught their eyes or a specific splash of color. Thus far, I've been visited by the newspaper delivery lady, who stopped her rounds at 6:30 on a recent Sunday morning to inquire about the heart-shaped leaves in the front yard. "They're caladiums," I responded. Another neighbor's adult children stopped over to ask about the coleus. As different perennials go in or out of bloom, I get a few "one-timers" who want to ask about the patch of color that came or went so fast. And I get the occasional visitor that really wants to know how much "work" all of this beauty takes.

A few years ago, I decided that I'd tell anyone who asked that my garden took no work but instead provided much satisfaction. I admitted that I was quite active when in the garden, but noted the activity was one of joy. "I don't work in the garden," I'd tell them, "but I do come out to play in the garden."

In a recent conversation with a fellow gardener, I heard the word "spiritual" used when discussing the gardening activity. This gardener admitted to feeling closer to God when in the garden than while being anywhere else. Mention was made of witnessing the entire life-cycle in a season, of procreation (propagation), of growth, of decline, and of death. Knowing that some plants can go from seed to seed in a month's time, I just nodded.

One of the more meaningful visits I had recently was from an elderly couple I had gotten to know. They were "walking the neighborhood one last time" last weekend, as they were relocating to a retirement home just a few days later. They had been in the neighborhood for 11 years and noted what a beautiful neighborhood it was. They noted how they really enjoyed passing by my place because it was always so colorful. They said they would miss their walks in the neighborhood the most, but that they decided it was time to make "one final move for their most senior years, before it was time to go upstairs."

I decided then and there that my garden matters.

The Second Best Time

July 2012

This last month has not been a particularly good one for trees. Storms blanketed much of the Midwest and the Mid-Atlantic states. And trees were often the victims of lightning strikes, high winds, hail, and sudden micro bursts, which led to loss of life and caused much destruction. In the West, trees were also stressed by wildfires. In Colorado, Wyoming, Idaho, New Mexico, and some surrounding states, wildfires took their toll on thousands of acres of national forests, as well as on homes in many residential neighborhoods. As of this writing, some fires continue to burn. Over the last several weeks, trees have fell victim to storms and fires, and the drought that is spreading throughout the country. But for each tree lost to fire or storm, there were also victims among the surrounding population. Less oxygen was produced, less carbon sequestered. Tree canopies that once may have provided shade in summer and windbreak in winter were gone. Trees often helped with erosion control, wind protection, and water runoff as well; the void will be noticeable. Dealing with these losses reminded me of the Chinese proverb that says that the best time to plant a tree was 20 years ago, while the second best time is today. Perhaps, the day the last tree limb is removed, or the last ember is extinguished, will be a good time to plant a tree.

Something Old, Something New
June 2012

I recently had an opportunity to visit High Line Park in the Lower West Side of Manhattan. It was a Sunday morning after a hearty breakfast with old friends – the perfect opportunity for a walk. What I experienced was not only a new way to view New York City, but it was a new way to renew decades-old friendships. Indeed, I was able to experience both growth in relationships and growth in my perspective of a city at the same time. My childhood memories of New York City largely revolve around visits to an aunt and uncle who lived there. My uncle was a composer and his life was off-Broadway. Our visits consisted of watching the Macy's Thanksgiving Day Parade and occasionally taking in a Broadway play. As a result of those visits, I never particularly thought of New York as a green oasis of any kind. Yes, there was Central Park, as well as some other less famous neighborhood parks, but the sights and sounds of New York that stuck with me growing up were of crowds and concrete, traffic and blaring car horns, and the occasional theater marquee. New York was a nice place to visit, but I was glad we didn't live there.

When my friends suggested we visit Greenwich Village for breakfast and then "walk the High Line," I really had no idea what a transformational jaunt I was about to experience. Yes, I had read an article or two about this repurposed, once-abandoned, elevated railroad bed turned park. But what the High Line presented was a whole new way to view the city and a greater appreciation for my friends' increased awareness of the role plants can play in our lives.

Walking the High Line gives visitors the opportunity to see the city from a different perspective, often about 25 feet above the streets below. The plant material, a mix of small trees, shrubs, grasses and reeds, and plenty of perennials and wildflowers, set the tone. What you are witnessing is a rebirth of an old relic, with plenty of heritage. In the process, the city has also seen a resilience, as the High Line has helped revitalize the neighborhood and has quickly become one of New York's major tourist attractions. The blooming plants afford the visitors the opportunity to experience what walking down the middle of a large perennial border might be like. But this plant border is one and a half miles long and runs through the heart of Manhattan. Parts of the New York City skyline at times frame the High Line; at other turns in the path, the plant material frames the views. There are also occasional views of the Hudson River.

Truly this is a fine example of giving new meaning to the environment by embracing the heritage of the surroundings.

As for my friends, seeing their excitement for the High Line made the experience all the more meaningful for me. Jon and Lee always knew about plants, and Jon even got his undergraduate degree in biology. But for the past 30 years or so, these transplanted Floridians have raised a family in a New York suburb of Northern New Jersey that has repeatedly been involved with America in Bloom, and they have participated in their city's efforts to enhance that environment. They understand the mix of plants in a landscape – trees, flowers, shrubs, turf, and groundcover – add to the quality of life. They also understand that plants are much more than pretty. Whether it is enhancing the environment, helping to create a tourist attraction, creating an oasis in the middle of an urban jungle, adding to the economy, or even helping to revitalize an entire neighborhood they understand the power that plants can have for a city. Plants have added greatly to High Line's park-like atmosphere, and this has meant a great deal to "The Big Apple." It has also truly changed my perspective of New York City. I now can embrace the slogan that New York, New York, is the "city so nice, they named it twice."

Looking at Life in a Vacuum…
The Allocation of Scarce Resources

May 2012

From time to time I give a lecture that begins with a one-line definition of economics: the study of the allocation of scarce resources. I note
that we often think of capital as being the scarcest of resources, but in a
broader sense, time, land or other assets, labor, and any other commodity
for which we wish there was a greater supply might also be considered
scarce. For many of our cities, scarcities may include tax revenues, residents, adequate infrastructure, and employers that provide jobs.

A few days after my most recent presentation of this lecture, I found
myself reading an article about a community that decided to spruce up its
city hall as part of a city-wide improvement effort to attract more tourists.
The city began by removing all of its existing vegetation including four trees,
beds full of shrubs, and the turf which surrounded the building. When it
came time to install the new landscape, the city's planning director argued
that installing artificial turf, though initially more expensive than real turf
with a lawn sprinkling system, would be cheaper. Artificial turf was guaran-
teed for nine years and would never need mowing, fertilizing, or watering.
Artificial turf for municipal buildings is the latest in a barrage of efforts
various cities have undertaken, purportedly to cut costs. I have seen cities
which have been long known for their hanging basket programs switch
to plastic or silk flowers using the same arguments about being more eco-
nomical.

I have seen plantings at city entrances disappear, tree circles in sidewalks replaced by concrete, and planters go in any number of directions
from total removal to artificial plantings to being replaced by animal figu-
rines labeled art projects. All of these efforts were sanctioned in the name
of being better economics.

With every such effort, I have thought some decision-making body
operated in a vacuum. Certainly, if only dollars and cents related to pur-
chase price and maintenance were tabulated, one could see an argument
for savings being made if the shorter life of some real plants was compared
to the longer life of synthetic alternatives or if maintenance costs were the
only variable considered. Yet, one of the advantages of real plants is the
opportunity of a continually-changed appearance due to their continual

growth or in the case of annuals, even their death. Change often has been called the lifeblood of retail marketing, for if it weren't for changing tastes and preferences and changing styles, little economic activity would be generated, other than when obsolescence or failure occurred.

A constantly-changing landscape, filled with all kinds of living plants, may by itself become a tourist attraction. Annuals provide the opportunity to put a "fresh face" on a planting on an annual basis. Perennials offer a different look as they go through the growing season, as anticipation of their bloom window is followed by the bloom itself, followed by an interesting seed head or more interesting fall foliage. And trees and shrubs might offer a spring bloom followed by beautiful summer shade, handsome fall foliage, and even winter interest, depending upon the bark, the tree's skeletal structure, seed pods or other fruit, or other attributes. Yes, these plants might require some maintenance, but their seasonality does offer the advantage of a changed landscape, which by itself might generate economic activity in the form of shoppers or tourists.

Additionally, I'd like to offer the suggestion that real plants offer environmental advantages that artificial plants never will. Beginning with the manufacturing of oxygen, the use of carbon dioxide, and finishing with the sequestration of carbon, real plants act as "wonder machines," improving our environment. Real plants offer temperature modulation, helping to cool cities in summer and providing windbreaks to help reduce the winter chill. Real plants can help reduce noise, dust, water, air, and light pollution, advantages that artificial plants cannot provide. You see, plants are more than just pretty, and as challenging as it might be, all of their attributes should be considered.

In one U.S. Forest Service study of all of the benefits plants provided, it was found that for every $1 invested in planting, mulching, pruning, or watering of a tree, $2.70 worth of environmental benefits were recouped. The development of an economic model certainly requires that all costs be considered. It also requires that all benefits be incorporated. Life in a cost comparison vacuum might be cozy, but it is far from an accurate vision of the true meaning of life.

All that Blooms

April 2012

Throughout much of the country, spring has come with such speed that it has left folks questioning either what happened to winter or whether it's already summertime. Indeed, if my neighborhood is to serve as an example, the crabapples that normally bloom the last of April or in early May were at peak bloom with a week of March yet to go and are only now subsiding, depending upon the cultivar. At the same time, shrubs and daffodils that normally bloom in March and in April are also in bloom right now!

Even the later blooming hyacinths and tulips are already showing color. On top of this, I have a spectacular display containing a new pansy that successfully overwintered here in Chicagoland that is blooming like there is no tomorrow. Neighbors have already been commenting favorably about all the blossoms.

The net result of all of this flower power has been a spectacular array of colors that has allowed Mother Nature to compete successfully with many of the brilliant new advertisements that feature the most vibrant colors seen in fashions and home décor in a number of years. Indeed, some advertising moguls have been writing about the explosion of color in ads for all sorts of products, but these pale in comparison with the beauty that this compressed spring bloom has generated.

And a few local retailers outside of the horticulture industry, with whom I've spoken, have noted that customer traffic was way off; they're attributing this to the beautiful weather that has their normal group of shoppers otherwise occupied. Indeed, if my yard is an example, the pot of gold is outdoors right now, as my yard currently displays every color of the "Roy G. Biv rainbow" blooming on one plant or another. Whether from the trees, the bulbs, the pansies, the wildflowers, or the perennials, it is hard to focus on any indoor activity right now.

As I pondered this vernal excitement, I can't help but wonder what it might be like if this volume of color was the standard, rather than the exception, throughout much of the year. Who says we should just enjoy the calmness of spring's newest green but avoid the splash of color, as many of my neighbors do? Why do we settle for monotones during a normal spring, even if the hues change from week-to-week as the season progresses? What makes a certain color combination right and another garish? When are bold colors considered appropriate but otherwise inappropriate? Where do these garden "rules" originate and how do these mores become the norm?

The truth is Mother Nature has once again reigned supreme. Any rule we may think we've instituted about staged blooms, appropriate combinations, seasonal variations, or the like has been thrown out the window. All of this color is doing its own thing, no matter how we've planned or what we've been accustomed to seeing in the past. Indeed, her royal highness has taken charge! And what a glorious array of color we have to behold! Have a happy spring! Be sure to enjoy every blooming moment of it.

UNLESS

March 2012

"Unless someone like you Cares a whole awful lot, Nothing is going to get better. It's not." From *The Lorax* by Dr. Seuss

Through the $70 million investment from Universal Studios to bring Dr. Seuss's book, "The Lorax," to the big screen, millions, young and old alike, will hear the message that trees are important. Deviating slightly from the book, the movie is centered around a young boy, Ted, learning about trees. He is forced to deal with his nemesis, the owner of O'Hare Air, who would rather sell bottled air to people than have trees produce it for free. So, from the community of Thneed-Ville, which sports 96-battery operated Oakmatic trees that go from summer to autumn to winter to disco via remote control, Ted ventures to find the truth about real trees, hoping to find one he can bring back to plant, all to impress a girl.

The movie truly does have a great message about the value of trees. It sports some more general environmental stories as well. I have been assured by friends that even a three-year-old understands that not all is right when the Bar-ba-loots are forced to relocate after their habitat is destroyed.

The messages for adult minds are a bit more complex. We are challenged to reconsider our actions when told that people will buy everything and anything sold in a plastic bottle. We are challenged to consider the habitats that plants create for mankind and other living things. And we are challenged to plant a seed, treat it with care, give it clean water, and feed it fresh air.

Sharing this charge, I am happy to report that America in Bloom has been extraordinarily busy over the last month, albeit operating on a much more modest budget than that of "The Lorax" movie. Last month, I wrote about "something exciting to shout about!" If anything, I underestimated the excitement that the month would bring. Still, we've done our best to spread the word.

America in Bloom was very excited to debut the new "Discover Plants" brochure. This brochure, along with the companion PowerPoint® presentation, both are available on the AIB website, have really created some chatter. As of this writing, we have already distributed 25 percent of the copies printed thanks to the anonymous five-figure gift from one of our long-time Stewards. Indeed, folks are talking about flowers and plants in new ways!

In addition, several folks took up the challenge of helping to make the brochure go viral, as best as any printed piece can do. Several organiza-

tions have added news of the brochure to their communications pieces, whether printed or electronic. I know other stories are in the works.

Another organization, Ball Publishing, which has also been a long-
time AIB Steward, challenged me back. They insisted that if we truly wanted to have the best chance for the brochure to go viral, then I needed to
help them with a series of off-the-wall YouTube videos to help spread the
word. The videos definitely are not intended to appeal to our traditional
flower lovers, but are instead aimed at younger audiences who do not even
consider plants. All have a humorous theme about the benefits of plants.
Hopefully, this will help spread the word about plants, about our new brochure, and about our other AIB programs to new audiences. You can see
links to the three videos released to date on the AIB website, as well. And
more are in the works. Whether any one is to your liking or not, the great
news is these videos have already each been viewed by thousands of people.

Another bit of the month's excitement came from AIB's presence at
the Philadelphia International Flower Show. This was the first time our
organization has exhibited at any consumer-oriented flower show. We
handed out thousands of the new brochures at the show. Thanks to our
many volunteers, including board member Delilah Onofrey, judge and
board member Katy Moss Warner, and to judge Diana Weiner for helping to secure materials for and build the booth. Thanks also to the many
volunteers who helped staff the booth over the many long days that the
show ran including judge Diane Clasen and board member and judge
Jack Clasen.

Plus, judge and board member Evelyn Alemanni spoke to the
crowds at the show as one of the featured speakers. America in Bloom
was the theme of these efforts, and we've generated a long list of cities interested in AIB programs, as a result. To top it all off, America in
Bloom was recognized by show sponsor, the Pennsylvania Horticultural Society, as the "Best Achievement for Depicting Horticulture as a
Way to Create Community" at the show. Thanks go to Suntory Flowers, Peace Tree Farm, Costa Farms, Knox Nursery, Eckert's Greenhouse,
Taylor Environments, Kraft Gardens, Bruce Jensen Nurseries, Wekiwa
Gardens, Foliage Design Systems, the National Foliage Foundation,
the Florida Nursery, Growers and Landscapers Association, and to the
Pennsylvania Horticultural Society, itself, for their help with the exhibit.

All of these efforts led to an exciting month for America in Bloom. These
efforts, combined with reaching the February 28 registration deadline for
our 2012 National Awards Program for cities, have led to a busy, busy

month. By the way, we have 26 cities participating in this year's program.

As the Once-ler challenges when quoting The Lorax above, the stories do no good UNLESS the stories are spread, told often, and repeated to help educate others who may not know the news about the benefits of plants. To paraphrase The Once-ler:

> You're in charge of the seeds.
> They produce what everyone needs.
> Treat them with care, with fresh water and clean air.
> Grow a forest!

Anticipation: Something Exciting to Shout About!
February 2012

This e-newsletter column provides me with the opportunity to SHOUT about something VERY exciting!

While I have known about this opportunity for a few months, I didn't know exactly when it would occur. While anticipation has been high, I have struggled a bit in contemplating how best to get the word out, and how best to convey my excitement for what I'm about to announce. More importantly, I've debated how best to get you, the reader, as excited about this announcement as I am.

You see, this announcement answers one of the greatest challenges America in Bloom and indeed the entire horticulture industry have faced for some time. What I'm going to announce also potentially will help communicate the desires and the hopes of forward-thinking municipal leaders to fellow policymakers and even leery constituents, who might otherwise question their thinking. I also suspect this announcement could impact school curricula, businesses, and even community organizations, each with its own constituent groups.

As I've thought about this opportunity, I recognize that people still marvel in the power of "word-of-mouth." Certainly, if something goes viral with today's technology, the word-of-mouth gets accelerated via electronic means, and as long as it is good publicity, you could be talking about a communicator's dream. But analyzing what it takes to achieve viral status can be compared to yesteryear's word-of-mouth, only on steroids. Smoke signals might have been an even more primitive way to get the word out, but the story remains the same: it's all about sharing the news!

Another communication adage suggests that a picture is worth 1,000 words. It used to be hard to use word-of-mouth and show a picture simultaneously, unless you carried a photograph or happened to be standing next to what you wanted to talk about. Modern electronic communications allow you to e-mail those photos or even to take the photos with the same cellphone you use to spread the word. While it can be very expensive to share words and photos at the same time to selected audiences (e.g., think of a Super Bowl ad broadcast during the game), Use of technology can make the cost almost negligible in many instances.

Electronics have changed the way many think about communicating. Certainly, much of the news media feels the pressure and demand for speed that makes it difficult to deliver the news as they did in the past. Some focus on telling "the rest of the story" or even creating the story, through investigative reporting pieces and the like. There may be an assumption that folks already have heard the "news," even if they can't answer the details about who, what, when, where, why, and how.

Communicating the impact and details of "the story" has kept many news organizations alive, whether speaking of broadcast journalism or even newspapers and magazines. Does the printed piece have its place for modern-day communicators? Print obviously allows one to couple words and photos in the absence of electronics, and print allows one to carry the message away, which makes it a lot less expensive than handing out cell phones, laptop computers, or even e-readers.

Print can still be used to direct recipients to the Internet, either through written directions or QR codes, to view and/or listen to even more stories or photos or to conduct further investigations into a subject. And while print, today, may be challenged to claim the ability to let you "read ALL about it" on its own, print still can provide a great overview of a topic or a way to spark interest.So, what's this news? Why the discussion of "word-of-mouth," photos "worth a thousand words," modern communications technology, and print media? What's so important?

I am very, no, make that Very, VERY EXCITED to announce that America in Bloom has just completed the production of a new brochure titled *Discover the Surprising Side of Plants*. Through the generosity of an anonymous, five-figure donor, who has been one of our regular supporters of AIB since the organization's beginning, and with writing and design donated by one of our board members, we have produced this story, which talks about the functional benefits of flowers and plants "beyond pretty."

"Discover Plants" is a beautiful, full-color brochure, which highlights plants for friendship, for the home, for schools, for neighborhoods, for the workplace, for community, and for YOU; these sections of the brochure convey many of the research findings we've posted previously on the AIB web site (http://www.americainbloom.org/) under the "Community Resources" tab, and many of the benefits I've written about in recent columns.

But this brochure is really quite engaging!

One of the reasons for the excitement comes because of the interviews of countless individuals with whom we've shared various mockups of this brochure during its development. Initial feedback suggests that florists, garden center retailers, interiorscapers, and landscapers will want to inventory this brochure and share its message with customers; teachers will want to share its message with students; and industry employers will want to share its message with their employees. We also believe this piece will have relevance for park districts, for mayors and city councils, for service organizations, chambers of commerce, and convention and tourism bureaus – anyone discussing the merits of flowers and plants, plantings, and city beautification programs.

We have made the brochure available as a PDF on the AIB web site. (For best results, download and print this two-sided, in color, using the booklet printing feature on standard 8.5" X 11" paper.) For those that may want to use this information in the classroom or to add it to another presentation, we've adapted the brochure into a PowerPoint® presentation with even more photography. We are also making this piece available for ordering in bulk quantities through the AIB web site. I strongly encourage you to print it out and view it printed in booklet form – it's a terrific read! Once read, please share your copy with others. Also, please share this message about the brochure, so that others can read its important messages. We'd love to hear your thoughts about the brochure on the AIB Facebook page.

One further announcement, for the first time ever, America in Bloom has been invited by the Pennsylvania Horticultural Society to share its message of "Planting pride in your communities" with attendees of the Philadelphia International Flower Show, March 4 – 11, at the Philadelphia Convention Center. Through the generosity of some of our industry Stewards and the volunteer efforts of many of our supporters, we have accepted the challenge of attending our nation's largest flower show. Board member and judge, Evelyn Alemanni, who chairs our External Relations Committee, will be speaking on Saturday, March 10 at 1 p.m. Other board members and volunteers will be staffing the booth throughout the week. We will also be distributing copies of this new brochure as part of our exhibit.

Certainly, we're very excited to see the culmination of many months of work. We're trying an older communications technology, linked with some new twists. And we want to thank our donor and our volunteers who have made this come to fruition. We trust you will share our enthusiasm for this brochure, as well as the enthusiasm we all share about the many benefits of plants.

The Color of the Landscape

January 2012

One of the first lessons taught about color is that white is a combination of all colors. As such, winter's blanket of snow might be considered, at least in color theory, the most colorful time of the year for landscapes. For a gardener, perhaps, the snowy landscape might be the perfect inspiration to plan the spring and summer garden with the various colors yet to come.

While the beauty of a well-planned garden can't be debated, there is another kind of beauty that such a garden can also possess. Research has also shown that a school garden, for example, can actually help students returning to the classroom from recess stay calmer and focus on schoolwork. These students ultimately have improved memory and receive higher grades. A school garden, therefore, might be said to yield gold stars.

When hospital patients have a garden view during recuperation, they have quick recoveries when compared to similarly-affected patients without such garden views. Flower arrangements and plants can also help encourage patients. Perhaps, the flowers and garden views lead to fewer (code) blues.

In neighborhoods with well-planned and well-maintained gardens, crime rates have been shown to be lower than in similar neighborhoods without these gardening activities. The more gardens in a neighborhood, the lower the crime rate. The garden color is said to attract neighborhood activity and yield more social relationships among neighbors. The presence of this activity is thought to deter criminals. In addition, adding plants to the landscape is also the only home improvement one can make that yields a greater return than the cost of the improvement investment. What is the color of these landscapes? There's definitely added green and maybe some gold.

Elsewhere, we know that trees and shrubs strategically planted in the garden can provide an excellent windbreak, and thereby lower winter's heating bills. These plants might also shade a building from summer's sun, reducing cooling costs. These plants certainly yield some green in the pockets of the homeowners.

One of the great things about all of this plant material, of course, is that plants use carbon dioxide, sequester carbon, and release oxygen. Used throughout a community, plants can help clean the air, ameliorate all kinds of pollution (water, light, and air), help control soil and wind erosion, and help reduce the heat sinks associated with metropolitan areas. It seems flowers, plants, trees, shrubs, turf, and groundcovers provide a lot of green, but in a variety of colors!

As we begin 2012, we hope many of you are considering participating in America in Bloom activities this year. Enrollment is under way for our 11th annual community evaluation program with awards to be handed out in Fayetteville, Arkansas in September. Our organization will also be adding some new ways to showcase your community this year. Stay tuned.

Remember, no matter how you color your landscape, we encourage you to plant pride in your community!

As Winter Approaches, Why Not Dream?
December 2011

For many of you, winter may seem like it's already here. Perhaps cold weather has already settled in. For others, this fall has been long and mild by most standards. Here in the Midwest, we've just seen our first measurable snowfall, which came much later than normal, but two days back in the 40s have made it but a memory. Indeed, the real start of winter, at least according to the calendar, won't occur until later this week.

For many, winter is the time when we give our gardens a rest. After all, the ground is usually frozen solid, and it may be under the cover of snow. The days are short. And often, conditions make spending time in the yard quite a challenge.

However, there are parts of the country where the garden is now approaching its peak. A November visit to Phoenix to attend the National League of Cities' Congress of Cities conference reminded me that in Phoenix, landscape color is just now peaking. Indeed, October there is like May in the Upper Midwest for garden sales. Give or take a month, the same might be said for parts of South Florida and Southern California where fall is a "second spring." In these climates, the summer may be too hot, but the winter garden experience turns out just right both for people and plants. For gardeners, the Winter Solstice signals a time when the subsequent lengthening of days allows gardeners to spend longer evenings outside, to enjoy the fruits of their gardening labors.

In any case, whether you're allowing the garden to rest or whether you're into the more active gardening season, the shorter days of winter provide longer evenings indoors with time to plan. For many, planning might include making a list of items to repeat and a list to delete from the next gardening attempts. For others, planning considers a list of new items, which can be added or substituted for old favorites. For some, plans might even include totally new garden features, including new beds, new hardscapes, and/or new accoutrements to complete the garden experience. For many, it is a time to dream.

One of the dream opportunities is to contemplate how to make plants a bigger part of your life in the coming year. We know that plants offer so many benefits for people "beyond the pretty." These functional benefits might warrant considering plant expenditures in the same way you consider other assets. For example, if a driveway's useful life is extended because it's shaded by a tree, you could consider the tree an investment on par with new seal coating. If this tree also happens to shade the house from summer's afternoon beating sun or shield it from a cold north winter wind, the resulting savings in air conditioning and heating costs can be considered in a similar vein as a benefit generated by landscaping. A similar thought process can be used to discern the true costs and benefits of flowers, shrubs, turf and groundcovers. Benefits certainly can cover a spectrum of economic, environmental, psychological or sociological areas.

To take this dreaming a step further, why not consider the accumulated benefits derived if an entire neighborhood got involved in greening. If an entire block suddenly planted trees along the curbs, the resulting shade would likely benefit all the block's residences, as less heat would be radiated back toward individual homes. If the entire neighborhood planted flowers in some kind of coordinated fashion, it would signal to all that this was a neighborhood that cared, that was involved, and that was working together. Flowers literally could replace the security signs meant to deter crime. If an entire neighborhood adopted the local school grounds as a neighborhood park that just happened to have a school in its midst, not only would more residents get involved with the school, but students might have a totally different perspective on the educational process. Studies have shown that when this kind of experiment occurs, students also are able to better focus on school work, they achieve higher grades, and the school itself will likely experience less vandalism.

Wouldn't it be grand to plan the "what if's" should the entire city adopt a similar caring attitude and embrace the possibilities of a consistent environmental approach?

Chicago's former Mayor Daley had such a dream and Chicago became one of the greenest cities in America. Similar overtures have been made by New York City's Mayor Bloomberg, Boston's Mayor Menino, and Philadelphia's Mayor Nutter, among others.

Dream with me one step further still: What would it take for your city leadership to dedicate itself to investing in green improvements and also to care enough to see how the city stands up to outside scrutiny?

Measured against the ideal, how does your city compare to other cities of like size when it comes to floral displays, urban forestry programs, landscaped areas, heritage appreciation, environmental awareness, overall impressions and community involvement? This scrutiny really is no different than what a tourist might see or what a potential new resident might consider. This is also what businesses evaluate before considering relocation to your community. Would your city pass with flying colors? Or would a few new eyes looking at your city objectively suggest worthwhile opportunities for improvement?

This last dream is the opportunity of America in Bloom's annual national awards program. Enrollment is now open (until February 28). Whether your city is currently nestled under snow or quickly moving towards the peak of the gardening season, this could be just the excitement needed to see you through those short days of winter. Please offer us some consideration and dream!

In the meantime, perhaps, consider buying a plant for yourself for the holidays, or offering plants to relatives, friends and neighbors. Who knows, the investment you make might pay dividends from that first smile onwards.

It's Time to Give Thanks

November 2011

The Thanksgiving season is upon us, and it seems only appropriate to thank everyone in the America in Bloom(AIB) family for all of their volunteer efforts which allow us to plant pride in our communities. Certainly, kudos are well deserved in city after city to all of the volunteers who help make the AIB experience what it is coast-to-coast. We are an all-volunteer organization, and it is through the passionate efforts of all of our volunteers that we continue to make our country a better place to live, one community at a time.

Today, I'd also like to thank another group of players in this all too important effort. Yes, I'd like to offer special thanks to the plants, the flowers, trees, shrubs, turf, and groundcovers, that do their all-important tasks in helping to make our world a better place. And while you may be thinking that "pretty" is the operative adjective to describe these plants' effects on our environment, their contributions certainly go way beyond!

Witness a few examples from some of our own AIB cities in 2011:

Springfield, Ohio, was recognized by AIB in 2011 for its floral displays. The city focused on bright, pink and blue flowers to tie the city's displays together and planted hanging baskets downtown, on the Veterans' Bridges, and on the terraces at City Hall. There were also flower beds throughout the city. It was indeed quite beautiful.

But I wonder if the residents were aware of the other aspects that the flowers provided, beyond the beauty. We know that flowers attract visitors and shoppers, and I'm guessing the plantings helped welcome both to the downtown area. I suspect the flowers could have also played a role in keeping vacancies in the shopping districts to a minimum. There's a good chance the flowers helped brighten the mood of passersby, as well. And while crime may not be a big problem in Springfield, there is evidence to suggest that green spaces help reduce crime. All of these additional benefits, and they're pretty, too!

Another "Buckeye State" city, Bexley, Ohio, was recognized by AIB for its efforts in urban forestry. As the judges wrote, "Bexley is not just a tree city; it is a city that could be an arboretum." The city's tree inventory includes one tree on public property for every resident. Private spaces add more trees to the tally. The city's staff includes three certified arborists, who also consult with residents when asked. The city's tree commission has even published a book describing the city's landmark trees.

The trees certainly help create a sense of place and a sense of community.

While the residents of Bexley are justifiably proud of their city and their trees, I have to ask whether these folks recognize all of the other benefits these trees provide. Certainly, the air in Bexley is probably better for all of the oxygen these trees produce. And we know trees fix carbon better than other horticultural amenities, at least on a square foot basis. But these trees also help to shade the streets, which research has shown will help the city get a longer life for its asphalt dollars. Trees also help reduce air conditioning costs, from the shade provided, and a well-placed tree can even help reduce heating costs in winter. Trees help block the wind, which also will reduce wind-caused soil erosion. Dollar for dollar, trees are really great additions to a city's landscape. Oh, and they're pretty, too!

Sackets Harbor, New York, was recognized in 2011 for its landscaped areas. The main commercial street in Sackets Harbor boasts wide sidewalk plantings containing great combinations of plant materials. Merchants know this helps attract shoppers. Tin Pan Galley's artful landscape makes dining there a delight. Entryway signs feature the official village colors and are nicely landscaped. In addition, the Sackets Harbor Central School Community Garden serves as a successful educational tool for students, as they learn about different types of vegetables and eating a healthy diet. And since they share the produce with local seniors, the students not only learn from different generations but about giving as well.

While the praise is well deserved, the landscapes, no doubt, are adding other benefits to Sackets Harbor. Several studies have shown that street-side plantings can help moderate traffic flow, help reduce drivers' speeds, and can even help reduce possible driver rage, not that these are real issues in Sackets Harbor. Landscape plantings also can help reduce glare, both during the day and from car lights at night. And appropriate landscaping helps reduce water run-off, provides habitat for birds and other wildlife, and can even reduce noise pollution. Benefits galore and these landscapes are pretty, too!

Fayetteville, Arkansas, was recognized in 2011 for its turf and groundcover areas. (Fayetteville will also be the host city for our 2012 Symposium next fall.) The turf and groundcover recognition noted not only turf on golf courses, ball fields, and event spaces, but also recognized Fayetteville's restored prairies, wildlife habitats, and wildflower meadows. Judges noted that Fayetteville was investigating the most environmentally appropriate watering protocols, species selection, fertilizer options, and pest management programs.

While I know the folks in Fayetteville get it – after all, they've been AIB "troopers" from the beginning, 10 years ago, I have to ask whether all of the residents appreciate the added benefits of good turf and groundcover areas. Turf is an excellent oxygen producer, as a 2,500 sq. ft. lawn can provide the oxygen needs of a family of four for a year. Turf and groundcovers are tremendous at preventing soil erosion. Prairies are excellent when it comes to maintaining plant diversity and whole-ecosystem balance, and prairies can improve water quality. When you put it all together, turf and ground-cover areas are really quite functional, and they can be quite pretty, too!

So, as we contemplate our many blessings this holiday season, think about all of the plants that help our lives in so many ways. Yes, they can be quite pretty, but they are very functional in so many other ways. (For more information on these benefits, be sure to check out the AIB website at www.americainbloom.org and search under the Community Resources tab for the benefits of plants.)

Have a Happy Thanksgiving!

Ten Years of Memorable Symposia

October 2011

Certainly, over our 10 years of America in Bloom Symposia, we've had many memorable speakers and tours, and our recent 10th Anniversary Symposium was no exception. How many of these events do you remember? Here's just a particular memory or two from each of our symposia over the last 10 years:

In 2002, we visited Washington, DC, but we were headquartered in Reston, Virginia. We came to the area while the sniper shootings were still unresolved and arrived within a couple of days of the last shooting. Our opening Symposium session included one of the architects responsible for the 1964 creation of the planned City of Reston. He challenged us to remember the ecology of the site. That year's Symposium co-chair Katy Moss Warner, then President of the American Horticultural Society, also spoke and introduced us to the concept of "plant blindness," telling us the landscape needs flowers to be noticed by most, otherwise it's just a ubiquitous green that is never seen.

In 2003, our Symposium travelled to Chicago, Illinois, where we had great opportunities to visit the gardens of the Chicago Park District just across from our hotel. Then mayor, Richard Daley welcomed us and told us, "I'd like to say we plant flowers and trees because I like them. But it's hard to sell the City Council on something just because I like it. So, we tell them we plant because it's good for the citizens, good for the businesses, and good for the economy. We talk about reducing crime, helping students do better in school, creating more pleasant shopping districts, and the like."

In 2004, we visited Indianapolis, Indiana. The mayor welcomed us and showed us an inner-city tourism district that included a state park with a horticultural theme, the city zoo, the NCAA Hall of Champions, the convention center, and all the hotels and restaurants one could hope for. He also told us how horticulture played a critical role in the urban renewal of his city.

Our 2005 Symposium was held in Cleveland, Ohio, where we could see cluster dynamics at work. Within a 60-mile radius of Cleveland, 18 communities had entered the AIB contest within our first four years. More have become involved since. Indeed, eight communities in Northeast Ohio were involved in the tour that year. And we were welcomed by Ohio's First Lady, Hope Taft.

When we went to Eureka Springs, Arkansas in 2006, it was like we stepped back in time to the 1800s. We were welcomed by this small community of about 2,300 residents, which annually hosts nearly a million visitors, and we were given the key to the city. Incidentally, those 2,300 people protect over 900 structures in the city's downtown that are on the National Register of Historic Places. Eureka Springs residents told us of three less-than-successful and increasingly-more-expensive attempts at using consultants to help the city with its infrastructure planning and how they got feedback from the judges' comments in their three entries in the AIB contest.

In 2007, Rockford, Illinois was our destination. On tour, we were treated to a collection of city parks of historical significance, and the mayor declared that AIB had brought the city together like never before. Previously, folks had talked about the good side of town or the poor side of town, but Rockford's involvement with AIB had helped the divided city become a real community.

Columbus, Ohio, our organization's headquarters city, hosted our 2008 event. In Columbus, we visited the restored Franklin Park Conservatory and the surrounding parks and community gardens, toured the historical gardens of the Governor's Mansion, and toured historic German Village. We learned how horticulture can play a critical role in the efforts of a Convention and tourism Bureau and had a back-to-basics program focusing on each of the eight criteria.

Hershey, Pennsylvania, also known as Chocolate Town, USA, hosted our 2009 Symposium. We learned how one man's vision could build a candy empire, a historic hotel, exquisite rose gardens, a school with an endowment making it possible for anyone to attend, and a factory town that all could admire. We also heard the story of how a college student was able to inspire generations of medical students to give back to the city that was going to host them during their schooling, by organizing an annual clean-up day.

The Arch, the Gateway to the West, and the Mississippi River provided the setting to last year's Symposium in St. Louis. We learned about community gardening projects that helped landscape the city, feed its poor, rehabilitate criminals, and restore aging neighborhoods. The city's famous fleur-de-lis-endowed St. Louis Planter offered a view of container gardening on a grand scale. The planter was originally designed to line Kiener Plaza, which was next to our host hotel, but it has taken a life of its own, as it is now being adopted for other installations and by other cities.

This brings me to our Symposium in 2011. This was a great Symposium. I would personally like to thank co-chairs Katy Moss Warner and Tom Underwood for their efforts with organizing this year's Symposium. They delivered great speakers and great tours! We heard from both the White House Chief Florist Laura Dowling and from Ed Avalos, Under Secretary for Marketing and Regulatory Programs for the USDA. Joe Lamp'l, author and television personality, and author Dennis Snow offered phenomenal keynote presentations. It was indeed a great event, which afforded us the opportunity to look back, while at the same time allowed us to look forward, as we unveiled a new judging grid to go along with our new simplified list of criteria. I hope we see many more of you at our future symposia for even more memorable events. By the way, next year we will be in Fayetteville, Arkansas, September 20 – 22, 2012. Please be sure to mark your calendars – you won't want to miss it!

Life's Balance

September 2011

The balance of life is probably not understood by most species, even if they're part of it. And in reality, part of the circle of life goes unseen. In the desert, cacti, known as being efficient users of water, can also be a water source in an emergency. Some cacti provide protection for animals. Hares, small rodents, and other burrowing creatures often build homes near patches of cacti in hopes that the cactus spines will help thwart predators. And after all of that, cacti also produce oxygen and fix carbon, the part of the circle of life that remains hidden to most.

Elsewhere, depending upon the desert, palms, yucca, agave, creosote, ocotillo, sagebrush, and other plants provide shade for small respites from the day's heat. Plants are also a food source for some species and provide habitat for others. Again, these plants produce oxygen and fix carbon, helping to continue the circle of life.

Snakes may spend their days coiled in the brush or even underground, emerging towards evening to forage, thus playing their role in this circle of life. Lizards may be equally coy by day and more active in the evening, at night, or in early morning. Birds may nest in some of the plants, feed on the fruits of others, and/or become the food of others species. Thus the circle of life revolves, and life in the desert hangs in the balance.

In the urban environment, daytime temperatures may not be as high as in the desert, if only because cities are often developed in areas with more moderate climates. Yet, conditions may be no less harsh. The steel, brick, concrete, and asphalt jungles become heat sinks of their own making. Add to this the humidity, the pollution from automobile exhaust, belching smokestacks from industry, and the wastes of man, and the urban environment may be equally inhospitable.

Often the mix of heat, ozone, and inversion layers keeps night temperatures warmer than those experienced in the desert. Of course, the introduction of plant materials into this urban environment can go a long way toward helping to moderate the climate. Just as in the desert, flowers, shrubs, trees, turf and, groundcovers produce oxygen and fix carbon, but these plants also provide habitat, food, and/or shelter for many of the city's residents.

Again, life hangs in the balance that nature provides. Certainly, the primary goal of America in Bloom is to encourage the use of plant materials in the urban environment. We do this because we truly believe that plants are an important part of mankind's existence. People need to have both an active (be around plants) and a passive (have plants around them) relationship with plants. Though urban plants still produce oxygen and still fix carbon, there is plenty of research testifying to the importance of people-plant relationships for other reasons. (This can be found on the AIB website at http://www.americainbloom.org/ under the Community Resources tab.)

The balance of life may be different than in the desert, but this urban balance is no less critical.

If You Keep Digging You'll Come Up in China
August 2011

When I was young and learning to garden I'd often hear an adult say, "You know, if you keep digging you'll come up in China." Well, perhaps that is true, but I know now that a 12-hour plane flight will get you there a lot more quickly. Sure, there is a 13-hour time change from Chicago, and you cross the International Date Line in the process, but the 25-hour net time change going to China still beats digging a hole with a garden trowel.

Earlier this month, I had the honor and privilege to travel to China to see some horticulture and to speak at the Dalian International Horticulture Forum. My topic was "Beautifying Our Cities with 'In Bloom' Programs." The story of the entire forum was so pertinent to our America in Bloom audience that I have to share!

The forum was co-sponsored by the Dalian Municipal Government and the company for which I work, Ball Horticultural Company. The audience was about 220 mostly government workers from across China who are responsible for some aspect of municipal, provincial or national government, often related to social improvement, parks, business development, and/or agriculture or urban forestry. There were a few growers from large commercial horticultural operations as well. And there was a smattering of foreign government workers, including two Chinese women working for the U.S. Department of Agriculture as trade development officers and at least one Dutch government official.

After welcoming speeches from Dalian Mayor Li Wancai and Vice-Mayor Sun Guangtian, who also addressed "Construction of a world-class garden city," Ball Horticultural Company's Anna Ball (who keynoted last year's AIB Symposium) spoke on Trends in the American floriculture industry. Anna's big point was that unlike the Chinese market, which is mostly related to government landscaping projects, the American market was largely driven by consumers.

Next, Robert Dolibois, Executive Vice-President of the American Nursery and Landscape Association, gave a historical perspective of the development of the modern horticulture. Mentioning that the U.S. horticulture industry's history is not even 150 years old, Bob noted that much of its growth related to suburban life and urban sprawl. Most of this development has occurred since World War II.

AIB board member Charles Hall, Ph.D., from Texas A&M University, was the next to address the crowd. Charlie presented much of the information that is captured in his just-published "Economic, Environmental, and Health/Well-Being Benefits Associated with Green Industry Products and Services: A Review." We highlighted this paper in last month's AIB e-newsletter, and the paper can be downloaded from the AIB website.

I was the last speaker for the first morning of the conference. I began with the justification for urban beautification programs as evidenced both by Dr. Hall (above) and by the Knight Foundation's "Soul of the Community" study, which I have previously reviewed in this column. You may recall that this study proved that beautifully landscaped cities offered better productivity (higher GNPs) than similarly-sized cities which were not well-landscaped.

Then, I presented a history of the "in Bloom" programs from around the world, beginning with Ireland's Tidy Towns program in 1958; France's Villes et Villages Fleuris in 1959; England's Britain in Bloom in 1963; Entente Florale, now in 12 European countries, about 30 years ago; Canada's Communities in Bloom 17 years ago; Japan in Bloom a dozen years back; and America in Bloom, now in its 10th contest year. I explained the contest as it differs from country to country and offered the AIB contest, as an example.

Beyond the contest, I also explained that AIB offered an annual symposium, a "best practices" program, an awards program, a fact-filled website, webinars, a "Best Ideas" book, a monthly e-newsletter, and more! I offered that an "in Bloom" program, in many ways, was a community enhancement program, which encouraged volunteerism and resulted in civic pride. Following lunch, Stuart Lowen, who directs the marketing efforts for Ball Colegrave (England), presented "Flower Power – U.K. style." Stuart highlighted many landscaping trends and designs that have been seen in England's Britain in Bloom program and other decorating contests in the U.K. His photography literally opened the imagination to the world of flowers.

Allan Armitage, Ph.D., University of Georgia, spoke about "Ornamental Plants for Hot and Humid Areas." He provided an "up-close-and-personal" view of trialing and trial gardens and discussed the breadth and width of plant options used to add beauty to the world.

Adam Schwerner, Director of Natural Resources of the Chicago Park District, always challenges our thinking when it comes to plants. Here, he provided photographic examples of his work in Chicago and some of the ploys he has devised to get people to notice plants. The painting of dead trees in bold colors was surpassed only by the painting of soon-to-be-removed, but still living, trees in its ability to generate reaction from both City of Chicago residents and Dalian audience members. Adam's presentation opened the world of plants to the imagination. The Chicago Park District sponsored Chicago's winning entry in the first AIB contest in 2002, and they hosted AIB's second Symposium and Awards Program in 2003.

Shi-Ying Wang, Ph. D., a consultant who has been responsible for China market development for the Ball Horticultural Company for more than 10 years, spoke on how to succeed in the China floriculture industry. He stressed the need to be aware of both Chinese and foreign cultures. Shi-Ying was the event's main organizer.

The next speakers, representing three production firms, spoke on Innovations in Plant Production. John Williams, Vice-President of Production and Operations from Tagawa Greenhouse Enterprises, presented "Implementation of Spring Bedding Plant Production" and explained how Tagawa utilizes its 2.3 million sq. ft. of production space in Colorado, California, and New Mexico. Elin Dowd, President of Monrovia Growers in California, spoke on Monrovia's "85 Years of Innovation." And Gary Mangum, Co-owner of Maryland-based Bell Nursery, spoke of how his firm grew to supply 200 Home Depot stores in Maryland, Delaware, Pennsylvania, Virginia, North Carolina, Ohio, and the District of Columbia using a network of farm families as supplemental flower producers.

Day 2 began with Shuhua Li, Ph.D., professor of landscape architecture at China's Tsinghua University, describing traditional Chinese and Japanese cultural elements found in Asian garden design. Dr. Li's presentation touched on Feng shui, Buddhism, Taoism, and Hinduism and how symbols and beliefs central to each of the religions get replicated in the traditional Asian landscapes.

Jeff Gibson, Landscape Business Manager for Ball Horticultural Company, discussed the North American professional landscape trade. His talk, which described the installation, maintenance and design elements of the landscape industry, served as the perfect introduction to the three landscape architects which followed. The first, Doug Hoerr, spoke of "Chicago's Urban Horticulture." He told how a small project in front of one Crate and Barrel store provided the impetus for much of Chicago's beautification efforts and how a small stretch of highway running from the airport to downtown Des Moines, Iowa also had an effect not only on beautification efforts, but also on the itinerary chosen by many of Des Moines' residents. (Incidentally, Des Moines is also an AIB city.)

Michael Braden, Principal of California's ValleyCrest Design Group, addressed "Increasing bio-diversity in the built environment." His thought-provoking comments about man's impact and potential influence on the landscape challenged all to consider the responsibility each has for environmental stewardship.

The conference's final speaker was Jeffrey Bruce, owner of Jeffrey L. Bruce Company, a national landscape architectural firm in North Kansas City, Missouri. Jeffrey invited the audience to dream with him about "The Future of Green." His talk catapulted the listener from considering the landscape around a building to considering the possible landscape on a building (e.g., green roofs and vertical green walls) and again to the possibility that a building, one day, might be made of live plants. This was indeed quite thought-provoking.

Following lunch, the entire conference group, speakers, and audience, hopped busses to tour Dalian's beautiful city landscape and then to travel, with police escort, to Pulandian, another city about 90 minutes north. There, the group was welcomed by balloons and Chinese drums, flutes, and dragons at the opening of the Dalian International Flower New Variety Show and Trade Fair. We also helped inaugurate a brand new city park, completed just that morning, and we were treated to a closing banquet. The press coverage for these horticultural events was unbelievable!

This trip, like other overseas and some domestic destinations before, reinforced my belief that what we do in America in Bloom is indeed important to cities and the people who live in them. Flowers greeted us at the airport when we landed in Beijing. Flowers and plants welcomed us as we travelled from city to city, and indeed plants blanketed almost the entire highway leading from Dalian to Pulandian, a 90-minute trip. As an ode to horticulture, fruits and vegetables remain a staple part of the Chinese diet and may indeed be the most recognized parts of the meal. In the blocks of the cities abandoned for urban renewal, ornamental horticulture was often the only harmonizing element. And when new construction enticed the views of passers-by, it was the flowers and plants that exclaimed we're open for business.

Throughout the week, most all of the travelers, and indeed even the conference's Chinese attendees, were exposed to new cultures and differences. But what brought us together during the conference was the discussion of flowers and plants, trees and shrubs, turf and groundcovers, the tangible elements of the "in Bloom" programs.

Even without interpreters, you could tell folks appreciated the "pretty" that plants bring to the world, but you knew the special beauty of plants is that their beauty encompasses so much more than pretty.

Capital Ideas

July 2011

We're throwing a party!

Yes, America in Bloom is 10 years old and we feel like celebrating!

To mark the occasion, our 10th Anniversary Symposium & Awards Program, October 6 – 8, is returning to the Washington, D.C. area, the site of our first symposium, and boy do we have a program planned for you.

Under the careful direction of our AIB Board member and judge, Katy Moss Warner, President Emeritus of the American Horticultural Society (AHS), and Tom Underwood, the AHS Executive Director, who are serving as Co-Chairs of this year's Symposium, we have something truly special planned. We're doing things a bit differently for the occasion, with some special guests, some special venues, some special features, and, we hope, you!!!

We're opening the festivities Thursday evening with a special banquet event at the AHS Headquarters at George Washington's River Farm in Alexandria. While we will present the Criteria Awards at this event, the venue will also allow for a great display of floral beauty, as many varieties ideal for urban landscapes will be featured, along with some creative ways to use these plant materials. The AHS Horticulturist, James Gagliardi, will be on hand to help guide you through the gardens. A special guest this evening will be Laura Dowling, the White House Chief Florist.

On Friday morning, author and PBS television personality Joe Lamp'l will provide the keynote address on Growing Greener Communities. Then we will break into concurrent sessions covering topics from building a healthy tree canopy to the power of flowers. AIB will introduce our new Showcase of Innovation, which will provide attendees with a quick synopsis of each exhibitor's products and services as a teaser for later investigations.

A panel of mayors will then describe how AIB has affected each of their communities opposite another panel describing the role of foundations in beautification efforts, in another round of concurrent sessions. Friday afternoon will feature area tours ranging from the U.S. Botanic Garden to the Enid Haupt Garden at the Smithsonian and from the many area monuments to the U.S. Capitol. All tours will end at the U.S. Botanic Garden at the base of Capitol Hill for refreshments. A guided walking tour of Old Town Alexandria will follow. Friday evening, attendees will have an evening on their own, in our nation's capital.

Our Saturday morning keynote address will be delivered by Dennis Snow, a former employee trainer at Disneyworld. Dennis will share tips from his two books, "Lessons from the Mouse" and "Unleashing Excellence: The Complete Guide to Ultimate Customer Service." The presentation is sure to offer inspiration for any business, organization or community in attendance.

The rest of the morning will be filled with concurrent sessions offering topics ranging from using social media to encourage community involvement, to growing healthy communities, and from energizing kids and communities through school gardens, to making the case for sustainable landscape solutions. We will also introduce our new AIB evaluation form, which will incorporate many recommendations that have been garnered from our first 10 years of city evaluations.

Saturday afternoon will focus on sharing ideas, commencing with our ever-popular Best Ideas Luncheon facilitated by board member and judge Evelyn Alemanni followed by sessions hosted by the judges who evaluated the various population categories in the 2011 competition. Both events are open to all Symposium attendees.

Saturday evening will feature the grand finale banquet and awards ceremony, honoring all of the cities which participated in this year's competition. We will also honor the John R. Holmes III Community Champion nominees and announce this year's winner. Undersecretary of Agriculture Ed Avalos will be our Honored Guest at this banquet.

All in all, this year's Symposium should be something quite special and will certainly be a can't-miss opportunity for anyone who cares about horticulture, people or community. It is definitely the highlight of our AIB educational year and a great way to learn more about planting pride in our communities. I look forward to seeing everyone there.

Life Lessons: Starting to Garden

June 2011

When I was six, my father led me to the side of our rented house and gave me my first lesson in gardening. We were planting tomatoes, and I learned about spacing, staking, and exposure. Years later, I still plant tomatoes. 'Better Boy' has replaced 'Burpee Big Boy,' 'Beefmaster' has replaced 'Beefsteak,' and the cherry tomatoes now are named varieties 'Juliet' and 'SunSugar.'

The gardening lessons of my childhood have stood the test of time. I have definitely branched beyond tomatoes, but many of the vegetables and flowers I now plant, I first experienced growing in my father's garden. When I was eight, we moved to a new home, which is still in the family. The somewhat larger garden there has been home to flowering trees and shrubs, a larger lawn, annuals and perennials, a couple of fruit trees, and a larger vegetable garden. Everything from asparagus to zucchini has been planted and harvested, though there has not always been a direct correlation between seeds sown and produce harvested; alas, the garden has taught so many lessons in this regard.

Indeed, throughout the years, horticulture has taught so many lessons. I learned biology, whether relating to the plants I was growing or the pests that challenged the harvest. I learned a bit of arithmetic, whether from counting seeds or space devoted to a crop, whether from calculating germination rates or yields, or whether from measuring the height certain tomato plants grew relative to the stakes used to rein them in place.

I learned some chemistry, whether relating to the Nitrogen, Phosphorous, or Potassium in fertilizers used or to the oxidation that occurred when metal and dirt combined with a bit of moisture to leave a rusty edge on a tool. I even learned some Latin, as well as some English, some history and some art, as I studied plants and their names, their backgrounds, and their use.

The garden has also taught me many life lessons. I learned a great deal about the senses and each sense's role in defining the moment. There is nothing sweeter than the feeling you get from moving warm, friable soil around a plant with your bare hands and tasting the fruits of your labors a couple of months later! I certainly learned about patience. And humility. About risk and reward. I developed friendships through the garden as well, whether it was the neighbor who worked in a local greenhouse or one of my dad's business partners, who was a landscape architect by training.

The garden has made me appreciate both Mother Nature and nature, the force, and the surroundings. I learned about cause and effect, about effort expended and harvests reaped. There was indeed a great satisfaction achieved when my mother asked if there was something in the garden she could use for dinner and I had something to contribute. Gardening also taught me about heritage, whether relating to the derivation of the cultivars I now use, the tutelage of my father sharing those first gardening lessons, the first vegetable and fruit cooking lessons shared by my mother (e.g., pumpkin pie filling made from my own pumpkins, which eventually led to a pie after hours of cooking down the pumpkin flesh), or even the Sedum plants that my father's mother contributed to the garden, which still bloom every August into September.

Gardening has indeed provided a lifelong reward. It was something my father first shared, and over 50 years later, our weekend phone calls often still include a few minutes of conversation about what each has planted or harvested, what has bloomed early or late, and whether the past week's weather has helped or hurt the garden's progress. It's easy being passionate about gardening, when I consider, in its own little way, the garden has provided so much beauty to the neighborhood, to the homestead, and especially to life.

Happy Summer!

Recognition

May 2011

"Don't worry when you are not recognized, but strive to be worthy of recognition." ~Abraham Lincoln

As America in Bloom celebrates the year of its 10th anniversary, the Board of Directors, our judges, our volunteer staff, and our countless other volunteers have been extremely busy preparing for the contest, conducting webinars, planning for the 10th Anniversary Symposium & Awards Program (October 6-8 in Washington, DC), preparing for yet another edition of our Best Ideas Book, and doing the many things we always do: spreading the word about our program and about the value of plants to cities and their residents. Some of us – those on the Board of Directors especially – also get involved in fundraising efforts, and when we do, the word "recognition" often permeates the conversation.

In the context of these discussions, "recognition" often comes up when a target donor is asked for a contribution, and we promptly talk about how the donor will be recognized. Our AIB Fundraising Committee has been grappling with updating our "donor grid" for the last six months so that we can continue to attract funds to grow the program. Our office will be happy to discuss donations at any time with anyone willing to write a check. :)

At other times, the word "recognition" swirls in our cognitive spaces as we realize the person with whom we are talking has never heard of our organization. Believe me, it is a humbling experience when you know you've been around for 10 years and find there are still folks involved with horticulture, urban beautification, and/or public works or park programs who have never heard about America in Bloom. You sometimes feel reassured when you talk to a hobbyist who knows the program well and what it has meant for his or her city or the next community down the road. But you still scratch your head every time you meet someone who should know about the program and all they do is return a blank stare.

Recognition is indeed a fickle friend. From one perspective, as a child I was always taught that the greatest charity was the donation given anonymously. Yet, I know that many non-profit organizations practically call for a herald of trumpets, depending upon the publication of their donor list, for its coercive effects in helping to convince others to join the bandwagon. Of course, a truly good organization accommodates the desires of all of its donors, who may alternately desire recognition or anonymity.

In the end, the best organizations keep their eye on their missions and know they are doing good work, even if the world has yet to learn who is behind the progress. As we continue our celebration of America in Bloom's 10th Anniversary year, please help us continue to spread the word, feel free to line up to offer a donation :), and help us continue to plant pride in our communities!

What's in it for Business?

April 2011

A recent discussion surprised me. The question asked was, "Why should a business get involved with a non-profit organization, from a business perspective?" I have pondered the question for a number of weeks.

Quite notably, the topic of being a "good corporate citizen" is in the news. There is a new web site,http://www.goodcorporatecitizen.com/, which suggests that, though money matters, today's businesses are finding that investors, customers, and employees want to be involved with companies that consider the environment, community activism, health, and safety in what they do. The Center for Corporate Citizenship at Boston College notes that 30 percent of businesses recognize that good corporate citizenship helps recruit and retain good employees. Good corporate citizens maintain high ethical standards, decrease the company's negative effects on the environment, and give back to the community.

Good relations aside, I still pondered what would motivate a company to get involved with a non-profit organization such as America in Bloom. Calling on my marketing background, I examined those famous Four Ps of Marketing, the so-called "marketing mix variables" for a clue. The Four Ps – Products (and Services), Price, Place (i.e., Distribution), and Promotion – have been the subject of many business books and articles, but I've always had my own appreciation of what many call a theoretical approach to marketing, as I constantly find real-world examples to support the validity of the concepts.

On a product and/or service level, one could argue a business might get involved with a non-profit because there is some affinity with the owners or managers or even employees with the products or services involved. In the AIB example, we might easily understand why a horticultural firm might get involved to demonstrate leadership or expertise, for example, but we might have to look deeper when a non-horticultural firm expresses interest. Perhaps, someone in management at such a company likes to garden. Or maybe the offices face a city park. Looking for the "affinity connection to the products or services" is the key.

When considering "Place," we typically talk about distribution. For consumer goods, we might talk about types of outlets, such as discount stores vs. boutique "carriage trade" retailers. For a non-profit like AIB, distribution might relate more to helping a firm transmit an image. Initially, we might find a firm getting involved with AIB for what might seem like a quirk of fate. Yet, such a business partner may choose to "connect" due to timing, as if to say your organization was in the right place at the right time to help our company disseminate a message. We often hear of firms creating a cancer fund drive at a time when a valued employee gets diagnosed with cancer. These firms often donate to a local hospital's cancer ward or a nearby cancer research center. Is there a right place/right time possibility for attracting firms to help support an AIB effort? Firms needing to testify to or to reinforce a belief in the local community, firms needing to demonstrate a concern for the local environment, firms wanting to claim a leadership role in the civic affairs of the community or those already considered "good corporate citizens" are likely candidates, and so too are their leaders.

Publicity, public relations, and advertising are all part of Promotion, and we'll have to admit some firms just get involved for the goodwill that might accrue to the product, service, firms, or employees of the business. Perhaps, a firm will garner attention for being involved with the community. And good public relations that may result can create an affinity between consumers and that company for its products or services. That could translate into a nice win:win for both the community, which gains the volunteer hours of a firm's employees, and for the involved firm, that can gain followers while building morale among the employees.

Whereas connecting to the charity's product or service niche is an easy link for some businesses, others may benefit more by showing involvement with a cause that its customers, investors, or even employees value. In this vein, a horticultural business provides an obvious link to a city's AIB movement. But don't be afraid to talk to businesses that want a little publicity about investing in a city's neighborhoods (e.g., realtors), in the downtown business district (e.g., banks, merchants associations, etc.), in the city's tidiness (e.g., waste haulers, painting companies, construction companies, etc.), or in the city's heritage (e.g., museums, newspapers, magazines, restoration firms, etc.). In contrast, any type of firm whose employees lunch at a nearby park could support the park district's efforts in honor of their employees.

The fourth "P" is Price. Price distinguishes the "buy" relative to other opportunities. Does a certain charity guarantee "better exposure on a per-dollar- contributed" basis or on a per hour of volunteer effort, all other things being equal? If so, that charity likely will benefit from corporate generosity more than others. Certainly one should also consider the type of exposure for the volunteer hours or dollars expended. One photo of a check being presented to a local charity may not stack up as well as neighbors seeing volunteers from a certain company week in and week out, out and about throughout the city's neighborhoods, helping to plant or care for flowers, collect litter, trimming the landscape, and/or helping with renovations, all activities which could be part of an AIB effort.

One of the keys to understanding the "Four Ps of Marketing" is to realize that the Four Ps all interact. A firm's opportunity for contributing a certain amount of time, energy, or money may be related more to a seasonal opportunity where promotion is king but which might look very different at a different price point in other seasons. This could relate to when their peak production and/or selling season (consumption) occurs, or not. The key, of course, is understanding what a business's motivations are. Getting the business to connect to your program's goals may be a piece of cake or quite the challenge. In any case, recognizing that businesses are part of the community and having the businesses recognize this as well, is fundamental to your success in approaching these businesses for help. Finally, you have to remember that if you don't ask, a lot of businesses just won't volunteer.

Don't be afraid to ask, and be prepared in case they ask, "How can we help?" Know whether man hours or money or even plant material is what you'd really like to see contributed. And don't give up should the first few refuse to help.

Good luck! Planting pride in our communities is the goal. Having the entire community involved is the key. And having businesses understand that they can be recognized for their charitable contributions of time, energy, and dollars might be just the carrot your community effort may need.

Lesson 1: Planting the Seed
March 2011

I have often written my column for the March AIB e-newsletter close to the first day of spring, and this March is no different. For this issue, I often find myself waxing about the birds and the bees, the relative warmth after a cold, snowy winter, or the first blooms of spring. Having seen the first crocus blossoms of this spring just this afternoon, I find myself fighting the urge to do the same this time. Yet, instead, I feel the need to write about my hopes for next spring.

On a flight earlier last week, I engaged the young woman seated next to me, asking her what drew her to buy the Better Homes and Gardens magazine she was reading. I wanted to know whether it was the cover photo, a particular article highlighted on the cover, a regular read, or something else. She replied she was an art teacher and she wanted the magazine to help with an art project, as it would provide fodder for the collages a friend was making for a fundraising project. She was reading the magazine first, but ultimately the pages would be chopped into smaller pieces and used for art. Intrigued about her classroom instruction, I asked her where she taught, what grades she taught, her favorite types of art, and the preferences of her students. I asked her if she ever used real gardens for her art subjects. When she said, "No, but that's funny, because I love gardens and gardening," I found my opening.

I explained that gardens and schools should go hand-in-hand, because there were numerous research studies suggesting that students exposed to green spaces did better in school. I explained that it had been shown that students were more focused on their studies, less distracted, more creative, and achieved higher grades when exposed to green spaces as part of their school day. Students also were more sociable, less prone to arguments, fights, or violence, and more "well adjusted" when exposed to these environments on a regular basis.

The art teacher and fellow passenger seemed quite intrigued with what I was saying. So, I explained America in Bloom to her. I invited her to visit our AIB web site to learn more and to also see the citations of research findings found on the site's resource pages. I gave her an AIB card with the web site address on it. And I asked whether she knew the right people to help make AIB a reality for her city. She responded that if she didn't know them directly, she had their children in her art classes. I asked her to picture what it might be like to have her school building transported to the middle of a garden, to have horticulture incorporated into her art curriculum, as well as into the reading, math and science curricula at her school, and into the curricula of all of the schools in her town. And I asked her to consider this educational opportunity as part of a larger community-wide effort. She responded, "You certainly have planted a seed."

Quite ironically, the very next morning, after returning to the office after a week of travels, I had a message to return a call. I ended up repeating almost the identical conversation. A greenhouse grower was looking for information to help prepare his community for the 2012 AIB effort he was helping to organize. And this is not the first community of which I am aware with intentions to participate in our AIB contest in 2012. I ask you all to help plant similar seeds for our AIB future. Along the way to helping to plant pride, stop to smell the flowers that this spring offers. They will be beautiful in many, many ways.

A Volunteer a Day

February 2011

For many communities, success in their America in Bloom efforts can be tied directly to the ability to recruit and keep their voluntary workforce. Indeed, one of our eight judging criteria is labeled Community Involvement, suggesting the importance of this effort. And we often get a lot of questions on how to best recruit the required volunteers.

Probably a standard approach to getting the needed manpower is to cast a wide net. Involving the municipal government, the business community, and a city's residents is important, especially since the judging evaluation for this, and all other criteria, awards points for each of these constituent groups. Yet, each of these groups ultimately needs to help recruit volunteers. So, the net that a city must ultimately cast needs to include every possible opportunity.

Certainly organizations, whether affiliated with the municipality, e.g., departmental groups of employees, schools, or even employee unions; with the business community, e.g., the Chamber of Commerce, the Main Street Merchants Association, or the Convention & Visitors Bureau; or with residents, e.g., neighborhood improvement associations, condominium associations, church groups, or PTAs can each provide a group of volunteers for the city's AIB efforts. And don't forget the individual approach as well, as some folks just are not affiliated. So, how do you make the right connection?

It may make sense to approach the volunteer effort as a marketing opportunity. Granted, some do seek out volunteer opportunities. (Some high schools do ask their more senior students to find a way to give back to the community, and scout groups may also encourage this. Some organizations may also want to see a record of past service before accepting a candidate as a new member.) But these volunteers may only provide a fraction of the force needed. And most folks really are not out looking for volunteer opportunities, so persuasion must be used.

As with all marketing projects, identifying the target audience(s) and the appropriate message(s) that will connect with each is important. You want your AIB effort to be top of mind when a prospect is ready to volunteer and again when a volunteer is ready to repeat the volunteer effort. And it is important to recognize that folks volunteer for different reasons; some volunteer for the recognition, for personal growth opportunities, for the sense of personal achievement, just to give back, to effect change, or to associate with a group of like-minded individuals or friends.

Given this range of motives and the breadth of groups you may want to target, one can see that a strategic approach to recruiting volunteers is important. For folks in specific neighborhoods or business districts, it may be easier to recruit these people for improvement projects in their vicinity. But if you need volunteers across town, organizing a larger work committee to handle projects relating to personal growth opportunities, working alongside the experts in a field in specific interest areas (flowers or trees or environmental awareness, for example, organized around the judging criteria), may be the key. In some instances, a demographic approach might yield the best results. Asking seniors to tackle the city's heritage activities and asking the youth to help with the beautification of the school properties, for example, might prove successful. In some cities, schools may even involve whole grades for flower growing and planting projects.

Businesses might be prime targets to beautify the areas around their shops or business parks, but if there is an opportunity to expose their business to new customers, they may be just as willing to volunteer in other parts of the city.

Contests can sometimes be an effective way to recruit volunteers as well. For example, finding a sponsor who, for the recognition, will gladly offer a prize to the service organization that generates the most volunteers and/or the most volunteer hours can be a win: win, providing recognition for all participating groups. In some communities, we have seen tremendous personal effort when the city, a business, a garden club, or even the local AIB organizing committee sponsors a home garden-of-the-week award. (Sometimes newspapers or radio or television stations can be recruited to get involved here.) This same recognition-and-reward approach can be used if the historical society sponsors awards for various restoration projects, if the Board of Education sponsors school gardening projects, or if the local sanitary district sponsors a collect-the-most-litter competition.

Of course, there are some folks who may just want to give back or those who really want to see their community change for the better. These are the true "saints" in the community. Often, identifying these folks and putting them in leadership positions can help the overall effort. Yet, even though their motives may be pure, they must realize that others with different motivations can also make good volunteers.

Working with all volunteer types, and making sure they have rewarding experiences, can help the overall cause. Another thought: don't underestimate the power of social media. If in doubt, look at the recent events in several Middle Eastern countries. These people reacted to the opportunity to effect change. While we certainly are talking about something less dramatic, the opportunity to recruit volunteers can really have a big impact on the community.

Finally, do everything possible to ensure your volunteers have a good experience, for their word-of-mouth can make or break your recruitment efforts. Volunteers want you to be prepared for their arrival, so their time is well spent. Welcome them with smiles. Offer training, if required. Try to make the tasks interesting – and for certain volunteers – a little challenging. Be sure to communicate as much information up front as possible, so your volunteers come dressed appropriately, bring the tools necessary for the jobs, and can plan not only their volunteer time but also the rest of their day. Make sure to communicate the appreciation, because most folks really want to know they are truly helping to make the world, and your little corner of it, a better place. For with the volunteer corps, you can truly plant a whole lot of pride in your communities!

Happy 10th – A Beautiful Bloomin' Anniversary Year
January 2011

Way back when America in Bloom was a fledgling organization, I remember a story told by the late Rance Searle of Bloom Master Corporation of Vernal, Utah. Rance told me that the people who sell disposable cameras were amazed to find there were more disposable cameras sold in the 7-Eleven in Vernal than anywhere else in the state. Rance said it was the power of Vernal's floral displays that sold those cameras. Not bad for this small community, considering the state has five National Parks (Zion, Bryce Canyon, Capitol Reef, Canyonlands, and Arches). Rance was always a big supporter of AIB. His partner, Marty Hanson, now the sole owner of the company, continues the tradition of support.

The reason these two gentlemen have been huge AIB supporters over the 10-year history of America in Bloom is they know about this power of flowers to welcome visitors to a town. Rance used to say, "It's like we rolled out the red carpet to welcome folks." If they were just passing through, they suddenly felt the need to stop and smell the flowers. Many bought the cameras to record their visit. Others decided it was time to have a meal, to buy a souvenir, or just to stretch their legs and enjoy the scenery.

Of course, not all green spaces have flowers. But flowers provide the cure to "Plant Blindness," the ability of people to be surrounded by nature but not notice it (first described by researchers Wandersee and Schussler in 1998). As Katy Moss Warner, now an AIB Judge and Board member, President Emeritus of the American Horticultural Society, and former director of horticulture for Disney World, told us at our first AIB Symposium in 2002, flowers were an essential element in getting Disney's visitors to appreciate the green space that was Disneyworld.

As we enter America in Bloom's 10th anniversary year, it is important to recognize how far we've come but also to recognize how far we can yet travel to beautify our country. There is no doubt that trees, shrubs, turf, and groundcovers are equally important horticultural elements. Environmental awareness, tidiness, heritage appreciation, and community involvement are equally important pieces of a city's quality of life. But flowers certainly do roll out the red carpet! And it is the flowers that accent the green beauty that all of nature provides.

Dr. Randy Woodson, now Chancellor of North Carolina State University and a floriculturist by training, gained much of his credibility as a scientist from researching the role of a plant's flowers in the life cycle of the plant. When Randy first discovered the proof that flowers begin to wilt when a plant's ovary was fertilized, I asked him what provided the clues that led him down this research path. Randy said, matter-of-factly, that flowers provided the invitation to pollinators to visit the plant. Once pollinated, he hypothesized that the flower's job was complete; for the species to survive, it was really better that the flowers faded, so as not to attract predators which might eat the plant. Furthermore, once pollinated, the ovary's role was to produce the fruit with its seeds to complete the cycle for the plant's regeneration. Randy went about proving the hypothesis.

Ironically, on a grander scale, flowers in a landscape serve almost the same purpose. Yes, they attract pollinators. But flowers also invite passers-by to stop and visit, to pollinate and fertilize the city's economy, to produce the gross receipts and the revenues that tourists, businesses, and residents need to keep a city's economy healthy and constantly regenerating. Flowers accent the rest of the landscape, so it can be appreciated for all of its contributions for enhancing the environment. And flowers provide the beauty that keeps the city inviting, which improves the overall well-being of all the citizens.

As America in Bloom begins to celebrate its 10th Anniversary Year, we have to remember that flowers are only one piece of a beautiful landscape. But what an important piece they are. For with flowers, we can all plant pride in our communities! Help American in Bloom celebrate its 10th anniversary year. Enroll now in the 2011 AIB Contest and plan now to attend the Annual Symposium and Awards Program in Washington, DC.

A Place Proud to Call Home

December 2010

We recently received a note about a study completed by the Gallup organization that was funded by the John S. and James L. Knight Foundation, which has created quite a stir. Called the "Soul of the Community," the study summarized the findings of 43,000 interviews over the last 3 years, conducted in 26 cities across the United States. Specifically trying to find the factors influencing passion for and loyalty to a community, the survey asked residents questions such as what makes residents love where they live and what draws people to a place and keeps them there.

The study provides empirical evidence that the drivers creating emotional bonds between people and their community are consistent in virtually every city. Furthermore, these drivers can be reduced to just a few issues. Surprisingly, the issues relating to jobs, the overall business economy, safety, and education were not at the top of the list. Instead, higher ratings were given to an area's physical beauty, opportunities for socializing, and a community's openness to all types of people. The study also showed that the communities with the highest levels of "attachment" also had the highest rates of gross domestic product growth. Hence, a sense of community and economic benefits go hand-in-hand. The study proved a link between employee engagement in the workplace, which has positive business outcomes such as increased productivity, profitability, and employee retention, and highly attached residents, who are more likely to contribute actively to a community's growth.

The cause and effect is not exactly clear, but the study found very high correlations between highly attached residents and their desires to stay in and contribute to their communities. The study found highly attached residents were more likely to see their communities as being open to many kinds of people. Attachment was also higher when residents perceived their communities as providing more social offerings and aesthetics they enjoyed. When residents enjoyed the communities' offerings, they were more likely to spend money on local activities and with local businesses.

Naturally, of particular interest to our America in Bloom family is the ranking of aesthetics. The study defined aesthetics as the physical beauty of the community, including the availability of parks, playgrounds, trails, and other green spaces. Though the overall correlation factor placed this in third place, 6 of the 26 communities studied placed this criterion in a tie for first place with the availability of social offerings in their 2010 rankings.

Another 17 communities placed aesthetics in second place, either alone or tied with the community's openness to different types of people. Aesthetics never ranked third in any one community's rankings, but three communities did place aesthetics in fourth among the 10 criteria considered.

In any case, this study provides plenty of fodder to suggest aesthetics are more important to a city's success as a community than some may have thought. Of course, we at America in Bloom have been arguing this point for some time. That's why our tagline is "Planting Pride in Our Communities!"

From Kids' Mouths...

November 2010

I recently returned from Halifax, Nova Scotia, Canada, where I attended Canada's Communities in Bloom celebration. While there, I developed a little callus on my forehead from changing hats, as I represented both America in Bloom and my full-time employer, Ball Horticultural Company. For AIB, I was proud to share some of the best ideas from our cities, as recounted in our "Best Ideas" book which was created by Evelyn Alemanni and donated to AIB as a fundraiser. The crowd seemed very receptive to the idea that we share over 2,000 unique ideas from U.S. cities, arranged according to the eight judging criteria in our book, and a number of books were sold. Order your copy of the 2010 edition of the AIB Best Ideas today.

As a representative from Ball, which sponsors the "International Challenge" coordinated by Communities in Bloom, I was proud to announce Warrick, New York, as the winner among smaller cities, and Zlin, Czech Republic, as the winner among larger cities in the competition. (Any city winning a population category in AIB's competition is eligible to compete in the International Challenge.) Warrick, which entered based on its 2003 win in the AIB competition, was only the second U.S. city to win this competition in either population category, and the folks in Warrick deserve all the kudos in the world, literally.

While sharing best ideas and handing out international awards is indeed exciting, perhaps the most memorable experience for many during the four-day event was provided by a group of junior high and high school students who performed a series of skits that addressed environmental issues. In the opening act of "MindShift," these students counted from 1890 to 2030 in five-year increments, as witnessed by a crew from Starship Earth, traveling through our galaxy. Crew members reported steadily increasing atmospheric and environmental degradation of the Planet Earth over time. In spite of repeated pleas to their captain that something must be done, the captain refused to intercede, saying, "We cannot stand in the way of progress." In the end, the Earth is destroyed.

In Act Two, the troupe returned to the present, portraying students, and provided a number of suggestions of what individuals can do to help reduce their impact on the environment. Suggestions were as simple as turning off the water while brushing your teeth and as complex as buying locally produced food to help reduce the carbon footprint from shipping cross-country. The message was clear: Shift your thinking and do something personally about the environment!

Many in the audience were moved to tears from the performance. In the exchange with the actors after the play, it was revealed that there are several different student troupes performing "MindShift" for 10th graders throughout the Halifax area, and the play has been playing since 2007. The play was originally written by a former high school student, who happened to be in the audience. Audience members called the play a powerful wake-up call, which effectively and almost too politely scolded adults to act before it was too late.

Several suggested the play needed more adult venues, and begged the author, actors, and officials from the Halifax Regional Municipality (HRM) to share the play's performances with others. To learn more about this play, see www.earthed.ns.ca/mindshift. "MindShift" is just one program that HRM has been doing as part of their Adventure Earth Centre. HRM's environmental educational activities have spanned the last 30 years and have reached 60,000 school students through a variety of activities aimed at different grade levels. (See http://www.earthed.ns.ca/ for more information about the various programs.) The Halifax Regional Authority should be congratulated on its activities in environmental awareness, as well as the superb job they did in hosting the 2010 edition of the Communities in Bloom National Symposium and Awards Ceremonies.

It's about Dollar$ and Sense – And About the Explanation
October 2010

Graduate students and student teachers alike often say they really didn't know a topic well until they were forced to explain it out loud to others. Certainly, I can attest that I wished I had experienced classroom teaching before I took my qualifying exams decades ago rather than after, as the exercise really helped me to understand the subject better than my student notes or textbooks ever could. In a similar vein, explaining a program can help overcome both one's insecurity as to the value of the program itself and signal the need to bolster the explanation of benefits going forward.

As I write this column, we have just concluded our ninth annual AIB educational symposium and awards program in St. Louis. And I find myself preparing for yet another talk about AIB. This one will be delivered in a couple of weeks at the annual symposium of our Canadian sister organization, Communities in Bloom. And while I think I understand the AIB program as well as anyone, it is the nature of the upcoming talk, as well as the interaction I had in St. Louis a few weeks ago with several attendees, that really makes me pause to reflect on the AIB program.

At the welcoming address at the AIB Symposium, I spoke about the benefits of plants, something I often do. I reminded the folks that plants are great for any number of reasons: First, some of us make our livings with plants. For all of us, plants provide beauty and contribute to the quality of life. I noted that plants can also add to the economic viability of a community, as they add to property values, bring in tourists and shoppers, and can help to attract businesses and residents to a community. Plants can certainly help improve the environmental quality by making oxygen, sequestering carbon, reducing erosion, and helping to deal with light, wind, noise, sound and environmental pollution. And plants have all sorts of documented social and psychological benefits including helping to reduce crime, speeding recuperation, helping students focus, increasing creativity, and increasing one's self respect.

I also encouraged folks to think about America in Bloom as a sustained effort, as opposed to simply an annual contest. We certainly are happy to have cities in our contest at any (or every) time, and we really want to increase this participation. But it is the sustained efforts of using plants in a community as a matter of habit that will generate the best returns for the community and its citizens. To that end, we'd like to congratulate the many cities which have adopted the America in Bloom ideals and made them part of the city's culture.

Quite ironically, if you look at our list of 2010 award winners, you will see that all but one of our population category winners and all but two of the criteria award winners were veteran participants in the contest. Believe me, this was not planned. Instead, this is a testament to the benefits that continued participation provides. Things do get better with time.

These benefits admittedly sometimes do need some explanation. It is not enough to say, "Plants are great!" Indeed when I first said it from the podium on the opening night of the symposium, and indeed on many other occasions when I begin a talk the same way, I often hear a chuckle or two. But when I begin explaining why I am so passionate about plants, folks often take notice in ways they have never before contemplated. Indeed, immediately after I gave that talk, a person from one of our repeat cities asked for a copy of the presentation. She wanted to share it with her mayor who kept questioning the real value of the program for their city. (Plants offer health and economic benefits.)

In my upcoming talk, I have been asked to discuss some of our best practices. After nine contest years, we have learned a lot from our cities about the various ways they have adopted our eight judging criteria. And just as our judges share ideas with each city they visit, these cities present us with various unique ways these criteria work in their locales. At our symposia, we have a number of opportunities to share the best practices among cities. But we've also assembled these ideas in our Best Ideas book by population categories, so cities can learn what other cities of like size do.

After a particular idea-sharing session at this year's AIB symposium, one participant shared that her mayor thinks the AIB contest is the best expense their city has in the entire annual city budget. Her mayor's stance was there was no better way to have the city evaluated than by having two outsiders visit and offer their perspectives, in writing, of what was good and what could be improved. Her mayor said the city had received far less feedback from several teams of urban consultants costing much, much more, which had spent entire weeks in their town. That is certainly a great endorsement! And it serves as a great explanation as to AIB's value.

Isn't it time to plan to participate in next year's America in Bloom program? It's about "Planting Pride in Our Communities." And so much more!

A Beautiful Legacy
September 2010

On Tuesday, September 7, Chicago Mayor Richard M. Daley announced he would not seek another term as mayor. When he completes his sixth term next May, "His Honor" will have served as mayor for 22 years, a record for the city and one that eclipses his father's record service by a year.

The City of Chicago, the Chicago Park District, and Mayor Daley, himself, welcomed America in Bloom to its second Annual Symposium in 2003. The Mayor was our welcoming keynote speaker that year. He told us that he loved flowers, but that, quite frankly, he could not sell city beautification to the City Council or the taxpayers on that fact. Instead, he said, I sell beautification because it's good for the city. Green spaces are not only good environmentally, but also economically, socially, psychologically, and more. News of Mayor Daley's decision not to seek a seventh term was the only front page story in the Chicago Tribune the next morning. The paper devoted two-thirds of the front page to a full-color, close-up photo of the Mayor from his tie knot up. Stories continued for the next nine pages as well as on both editorial pages of Section 1.

A stunning full-color shot of Chicago's skyline taken from Millennium Park, which was not yet officially open in 2003, highlighted page 3, with the title "Chicago reshaped, mostly for the better." (We did have some Symposium receptions in completed parts of that park in 2003.) This article highlighted many of the Mayor's qualities. Included in the list of attributes was he "...ruled Chicago with an iron fist and a green thumb, often using the power of the former to carry out the agenda of the latter." The article, by Blair Kamin, noted that during the Mayor's 21-year reign to date, 600,000 trees have been planted, more than 85 miles of landscaped medians have been constructed, and more than 7 million square feet of green roofs have been built. Kamin noted that, "All that greenery represented Daley's effort to transform Chicago from a City Functional, where utilitarian concerns were paramount, into a City Beautiful, where quality-of-life issues carried equal weight."

The New York Times also featured an article on the Mayor in the Sunday, September 12 edition. Almost every paragraph of Susan Saulny's article spoke of green spaces, parks, flowers, and/or landscaping. Saulny noted it took, "...a measure of willpower to transform the 'hog butcher of the world,' as Chicago was known around the middle of the last century, into one of the most forward-looking of cities, with an abundance of public art and green space alongside an ever-expanding skyline." These two articles, as well as many others from around the country, capture the essence of Mayor Daley and of America in Bloom. Increased green spaces yield an improved economy. Quality-of-life issues matter, and horticulture can help provide that measure.

Dominoes

August 2010

I recently read some newspaper coverage from one of our AIB contest cities which quoted a consumer about what America in Bloom meant to her as a gardener. Her response was, "It's great! It gives me all kinds of ideas about what plants to grow and in what combinations." She continued, "If it's successful on Main Street, then I think I can grow this in my yard, too."

Certainly, our experience is that when a city gets together to try to win the contest, everyone gardens. The municipality, the business community, the schools, the service organizations, the homeowner associations, and even individual residents all do their best to clean their properties, plant flowers, trim hedges, prune trees and shrubs, and trim the lawns. Some cities even get together to try to coordinate a "city flower" to be planted throughout the town, while others prefer to let each gardener express their own feelings through the flowers they plant. In any case, it's like polishing all of the band members' shoes before the big parade.

The learning opportunity expressed in the above quote – if it's successful elsewhere, then I can also grow it, too – is quite interesting. For many years, avid gardeners have referred to a "domino effect" that occurs in a city, neighborhood, or subdivision. This is often expressed as, "The more one gardener plants, the more it influences others to garden."

Yet, I have heard of many instances where one prominent planting in a city influences others to seek out that same plant. I recall a garden center manager commenting that a landscaper had planted a new showy perennial next to the entrance sign of the city's airport. For the month when this plant was in bloom, the garden center could not keep that plant in stock. Taken to another level, I know garden center managers who regularly seek out the plans for certain highly visible plantings ahead of time, so they can be sure to have specific selections in stock. This, too, is a kind of defensive "domino effect."

In many neighborhoods, one is able to admire the flowers that others plant. When everyone plants, everyone enjoys the view. But in some instances, gardeners may plant more out of personal pride for the way one's own home looks than for the self-enjoyment they might or might not get from neighbors' activities. This is when you really hope for the "domino effect."

Though not an official policy of the organization, America in Bloom advocates playing dominoes. So help plant pride in your communities. Get out there and garden!

Benefits, Books, Grants and Ideas
July 2010

At a recent Cornell University conference examining the horticulture industry's environmental impact, more than one speaker mentioned America in Bloom and noted how the program was raising industry awareness among cities, citizens, and public officials. I was particularly gratified to hear two speakers mention the "Community Resources" section of the AIB web site. The information collected here is not only aimed at helping cities with their AIB programs, but it also has turned into a tremendous resource for many looking for reasons to justify their involvement with plants.

The pages here are filled with all kinds of information which can help cities, researchers, or others understand the benefits of plants. These benefits are highlighted under categories such as health, economics, or one of the AIB contest's judging criteria. Every study relating to people: plant interactions of which we are aware is listed here, and we are constantly adding new citations to the information documented.

There also is an opportunity to order our newest Best Ideas book or to download and view an older edition of the book for free. The newest edition, released last fall, is already an American Horticultural Society book award nominee, and it is in its third printing. This book really can provide a lot of ideas for a community to benchmark itself against other cities' efforts and can help guide its own projects.

Another feature of the AIB Community Resource pages is the listing of granting agencies which have a history of providing funding for community greening programs. Some of these programs are aimed at city tree programs or other aspects of urban beautification. Others target school horticulture or youth garden programs or similar subjects. While some of the grants offer horticultural products like seeds or bulbs, others offer a different green input – cash.

The Community Resources section of the AIB web site provides a great way for a city to get started on the path to planting pride in its community. By coupling these pages with the information from other sections, e.g., the "Participation Toolbox," a city could be well on its way to providing its citizens with a more inviting place to live and work.

A Few Days in Colorado

June 2010

A business trip recently took me to Colorado, where I visited with greenhouse growers for the better part of three days. On my last morning, a slight diversion took me to the planting of a community garden. A local grower had supplied vegetable plants to help 13 different community gardens located throughout the city. The project worked with Denver Urban Gardens (DUG), a 25-year-old local non-profit dedicated to exposing people to the benefits of getting outside to enjoy nature, the Denver Public School System, and for this particular event, Burpee Home Gardens®.

The event I attended was at Fairview Elementary School in Denver's Sun Valley neighborhood, just south of Mile High Stadium, where the NFL's Denver Broncos play. During the planting, which was covered by the local CBS and NBC television affiliates, I had a chance to talk to the school principal, Norma Giron.

I could tell Ms. Giron was a dedicated and caring individual. As she explained the demographics of the school population and the neighborhood, I could tell passion was also a requirement to survive in this particular school and relatively poor (economically) neighborhood.

When she first arrived at the school 10 years ago, the school had no playground. Seeing an opportunity, Ms. Giron had a playground established across the street on the footprint of the old school, which had sat idle since the "new school" was built in the 1970s. A year later, a community garden was established on the parcel adjacent to the playground.

Ms. Giron recounted how the early days of the garden included vandalism, stolen tools, and graffiti. A few years into the project, however, vandalism of all kinds almost disappeared. Ms. Giron attributed this, in part, to former students who had aged and become neighborhood role models, who would not tolerate damage to the community's garden. In addition, since produce from the garden, which gets sold at the corner farmer's market, provided the only local source for fresh fruits and vegetables within a 10- to 12-block area, residents of the neighborhood felt an obligation to keep the garden productive and free from strife.

I asked Ms. Giron if she had detected any changes to the school or the neighborhood as a result of the garden. Answering in the affirmative, Ms. Giron recounted how in the early days, discipline was a bigger issue in the school. Parents would take little interest in the school or, it seemed, their children, most often ignoring requests for parent-teacher conferences and the like.

After a few years of interacting at the community garden, parents not only responded to requests from teachers, but parents began investigating ways to become more involved in the classroom. Needless to say, Ms. Giron was very thankful for the community gardening effort and its associated results.

The Denver Urban Gardens organization is quite special. For 25 years, DUG has helped to establish a network of community gardens throughout Metro Denver. DUG serves as a technical resource, helping neighborhoods with securing land, designing and building community gardens, supporting garden organization, leadership, outreach and maintenance, utilizing gardens as extraordinary places for learning and healthy living, and linking gardens with related local food system projects and policy. DUG interacts with over 32,000 individuals annually.

As I travelled throughout the greater Denver area, I detected a real appreciation for horticulture, one that I had not quite appreciated during any of the previous trips made there over the last 30 years. Surely, it was apparent in the inner-city work seen at Fairview Elementary. But I also felt this way during the customer visits made over the three days. In greenhouse after greenhouse, I could tell growers were readying planters, hanging baskets, and window boxes, not just for retailers getting ready to sell to the public, but also for any number of communities directly and/or for landscapers who had city contracts. In one such operation, I was told plants were being produced for a dozen different cities. Ironically, as I asked growers about their knowledge of America in Bloom,

I was amazed at how few knew about our organization. Indeed, I had been suspect, as we've only had two Colorado cities enter our AIB contest over the nine contest years. I knew we had a secret that needed to be shared. Perhaps, during this fall's National League of Cities' Congress of Cities, which will be held in Denver, the secret will be shared further.

But the truth is many Coloradoans already understand the power of plants in their lives. Certainly the folks at Denver Urban Gardens understand the power of plants after their 25 years of helping local groups establish neighborhood community gardens for all of the social benefits that gardening can bring.

School principal Norma Giron also serves as a testament to the power of plants and gardens to change neighborhoods and attitudes. The many Colorado cities that are already beautifying their entrances, their streets, their business districts, their municipal buildings, their parks, and their neighborhoods already understand the power of plants to help them be more competitive when folks look for a place to live, for a place to do business, or for a place to vacation. And certainly many of the people who choose to call Colorado home do so because of the inherent beauty of the natural surroundings. It just may mean folks are unaware there is an organization that can help advocate for city beautification with horticulture as its focus; unaware, perhaps, because beautification comes so naturally.

But maybe there are folks in Colorado or elsewhere that could learn about the special power of plants to affect their lives if only they knew about America in Bloom. So, please do us a favor and tell folks about AIB. Or just send them to our AIB web site at http://www.americainbloom. org/. Let people know about the power of both being around plants and of having plants around them. Let them know we can help them plant pride in their communities!

Texicali

May 2010

"Each time a man stands up for an ideal, or acts to improve the lot of others, or strikes out against injustice, he sends forth a tiny ripple of hope, and crossing each other from a million different centers of energy and daring, those ripples build a current which can sweep down the mightiest of walls."
~Robert F. Kennedy

I recently returned from a lengthy trip where I visited much of the California coast and Southwest Texas. As I flew home on day 16 of the trip, I began thinking about this column. Among the many e-mails that awaited my attention was an e-newsletter with an article about a Harvard college student who was running the Boston Marathon to help raise money for a particular cause about which he was quite passionate. His goal was to raise $100,000. The quote above was cited as part of his motivation. That is passion. I, too, was recently "accused" of being quite passionate. An acquaintance of many years, with whom I recently had come to work more closely, stopped me to say, "After all these years, I finally realize why I admire you. You are quite passionate about this industry [horticulture]. And you are passionate about America in Bloom." Guilty.

Asked to describe the cause of this passion, I could only speak to what I have seen over and over again. Plants do have a way of changing the environment, both literally and figuratively. In Big Bend National Park in Southwest Texas last month, the cactuses were blooming. If you've ever questioned the capacity of people to really admire flowers, then you have never seen a desert full of Prickly Pear Cactus in bloom being photographed by a group of grown men. Cactuses can really change a man, and they can also change the landscape – especially when they're blooming!

As I travel, I often notice two versions of the world around us. I see cities and towns unified only by the litter in the streets and the graffiti on the walls of vacant buildings. I ask myself how this much litter can end up in one place with no one caring enough to clean it up. The alternative is witnessed in cities with welcome signs planted (even with cactuses), streets that are litter-free, and businesses that are flourishing. Ironically, these two scenarios do not seem to depend on relative wealth or population, for I've seen examples of both in cities and towns large and small, with expensive looking homes and storefronts, and those much more modest.

Instead, what seems to vary in the alternatives is pride. In even some of the smallest of towns, the church often stands out as the best-kept building. After all, no one wants to be accused of attending a run-down church. And where the church glistens in the morning sun, there is no litter and the homes are planted as if to say, "I live here and I care." In other towns, the cemetery might be the "best kept" lot. Perpetual care can go a long way, but when graves are marked with falling and rotted crosses, even the signs designating the cemetery as being a special place cannot belie its character. This, too, is a reflection of a community's self esteem, but it is far different than the first. Really, like the radiating branches of the Ocotillo (Fonquieria splendens), especially when in leaf and in bloom, much of what you see is connected to how you're rooted.

When we at America in Bloom talk about "Planting pride in our communities!" it comes from real experiences. When we solicit your participation, it is because we know the power of flowers and plants to change men's (and women's and children's) lives. When we ask for your contributions, it is because we can't be too evangelical in spreading the word. We, too, have passion! Please join us.

Renewal

April 2010

In many ways, spring is the start of the year. After winter's challenges for our landscapes and, perhaps, our souls, the greening of the grass, the swelling of the buds, the first garden or woodland blooms yield a bit of renewal. In similar ways, our America in Bloom cycle takes off with spring's arrival. In many communities, litter pick-ups, spring cleaning, and planting new trees, shrubs and flowers, all signals of spring, herald that cities are putting out the welcome mats for citizens and visitors. As you read this, the horticulture industry is engaged in its main business season. In the spirit of renewal, spring is also the season that horticulture unveils its newest varieties. Whether totally new species, new colors, or improvements on mainstay garden favorites, the industry showcases its newest wares for all to appreciate.

The floriculture industry has its own version of its "curtain opening" in its annual California Spring Trials. Showcased at breeder open house locations spread from San Diego to San Francisco, the global industry introduces new breeding to the trade which will be available at retail a year later. Many of the new varieties have been "in the making" for five to seven years or more. And all vie for a little space in a producer's greenhouse, a little space in the garden center display, and a little corner of the consumer's garden.

Yet, the payback for any breeding effort is far from assured. A competitor's new variety can "scoop" the market just as a breeding company unveils what it thought would be a winner. Or the marketplace may welcome the new breeding with a "ho hum" attitude. Still, with all this risk, breeders worldwide vie for the opportunity to interest gardeners in their latest advances. Each hopes to win the hearts of gardening fans. It's all part of the horticulture's spring renewal. With each spring comes the query as to "what's new?" So, share the bounty – and embrace spring!

IMPACT!

March 2010

Someone recently asked me about the impact America in Bloom really has when a city only participates in the contest one time. He further challenged me about impact, noting the 20-something total cities in the contest over each of the last few years.

I proceeded to challenge his thinking by relating the story of Warwick, New York, a city that participated in the very first year of AIB contest in 2002 but has not participated since. We contacted an AIB friend in Warwick to ask why. In 2002, our friend, a local greenhouse grower, had brought together the owners of all of the town's horticultural firms, including her greenhouse, a local nursery, garden centers, landscapers, and arborists, to discuss what they might do, working together, for the city. Several of these owners had never met previously, and several viewed others as "the competition." My friend reported that the "Warwick in Bloom" effort was still quite functional. All 16 firms that originally had gathered were still in business. They still meet each winter to decide how to add to what they've been doing for the city. And every one of these businesses has grown its sales volume along the way. She was proud to announce their local effort had continued throughout the years, and that the citizens, municipality, and horticultural businesses were all beneficiaries.

This year, Warwick is competing in the International Challenge, sponsored by Canada's Communities in Bloom program, with which AIB partners. (Winners of an AIB population category can enter the International Challenge, in which they compete with winning cities from a number of "in Bloom" programs around the world.) AIB typically has at least one of its judges serving as an international judge for this competition, which helps our judges "compare notes" with other programs and their judges. This allows all of the "in Bloom" programs to exchange ideas.

So, the truth is that while we may have only 20-something cities in the contest right now, we have many more cities that are beautifying their landscapes based on past experiences and the continuous improvement upon which they build. Indeed, since 2002, America in Bloom has hosted over 180 communities in the contest.

Any many of these cities have repeatedly participated in the contest. After a recent talk, an audience member commented about a neighboring community that has participated in our contest over and over again. He assured me they did this for the judges' evaluations. "There is no better way to know how your city comes across to visitors than to get a written report from a pair of first-time visitors," he suggested. "And the value of that report is a real bargain each and every time." Indeed, the 20- to 30-page evaluation with comments on each of the eight criteria across all three judging sectors (citizens, municipal, and commercial) provides plenty of fodder for a city to use for this kind of continuous improvement. Mayors have compared favorably the AIB evaluation to expensive consultant reports.

In truth, the AIB impact is much greater than our city count or the 22 million residents of these cities. As I have noted in issues past, AIB often experiences a clustering of cities on our participation map. There is every reason to believe that additional cities see the transformations occurring in neighboring communities. In turn, these cities make improvements even though they may not enter the contest. The AIB reach goes much further than just the cities registered for the contest in any one year.

Accountability: We're Spreading the Word!

February 2010

America in Bloom has been spreading the word, literally, of late, and we've been spreading the word in ways like we've never done before. Beginning in mid-January, AIB was represented at a number of horticultural industry events. After all, we've got to keep the industry informed about our program, as these folks often become volunteers and sometimes even catalysts for their local communities. First, we were at the Tropical Plant Industry Exhibition (TPIE) in Ft. Lauderdale, Florida. Less than a week later, AIB was in Chicago at the Mid-America Horticultural Trade Show. And then, the same AIB trade show booth made its way to Louisville, Kentucky for the American Nursery and Landscape Association Management Clinic.

In addition to having our booth tour the country, AIB Board members, judges, and other volunteers have been out and about helping to acquaint cities and towns, citizens, and even students with the workings of our annual contest and symposium. Speaking engagements have been in as many locations as ever. And AIB conducted its first live webinar earlier this month which involved hundreds of registrants. Everywhere we've been, there have been questions about America in Bloom.

Some just want to know about the workings of the contest. Some ask more about the relationship between people and plants. A number have asked about getting a PowerPoint® presentation to help explain the organization and the contest to city officials, volunteers, or organizations. We have directed many folks to our newly updated web site at www.americainbloom.org for answers.

We've also had some more difficult questions lobbed in our direction. After a classroom presentation, one student asked why their city had not been involved in the program and why more cities haven't participated from their state. Hearing about the tremendous payback of city beautification projects in a number of cities' park systems, one person questioned why this story had not been communicated everywhere, as if the media had been negligent in doing their job. Noting the tremendous social benefits that have been proven to accrue to those exposed regularly to green spaces, a number of folks questioned why a lot more plants aren't used around schools, around prisons, and throughout cities.

Quite coincidentally, at a recent seminar on "Going Green," where the speaker had no connection to the horticultural industry or to AIB, the little-known parable of "Jotham's Fable" was offered as a reason why "others" were writing the direction of the "Green Movement." The story compares a Biblical tragedy to a time when the trees decided they needed a leader, a "king of the trees." Asked to serve, the olive tree declined, claiming it was too busy making the oil used to anoint kings. The fig tree also declined, noting it was preoccupied in its quest to make a more delicious fruit. The trees then approached the grapevine, not even a tree; the vine struggled with the thought, since it was focused on making the fruit that served as the source of both religious service and libations to quench man's thirst. In the end, the trees approached the lowly bramble, which agreed to serve as ruler, only to make the trees regret their invitation. This speaker suggested the true meaning of Jotham's Fable was to promote both leadership and volunteerism and to dismiss impotence and reluctance to serve.

Perhaps, in the months ahead, the true leaders of the "original green movement" should tell their story, specifically what being green means to each and every city in the country and what being green can really mean for the citizens. Neglecting to do this might allow society's brambles to rule. America in Bloom is telling its story. Are you?

Preparing for Class in the New Year: The Value of City Parks
January 2010

As noted in the President's message of another organization to which I belong, at the New Year, one often takes the opportunity both to look back and to look ahead. This might be deemed especially important this year, since we are embarking on a new decade. Yet, except for historical purposes and the possibility of learning the lessons from that history, looking back usually is not as productive as looking forward. Of course, good planning tries to take those lessons from history to help weigh options and forecast likely outcomes for the various paths which might be selected for the future.

One of my first assignments in the New Year is to prepare to speak to a class titled "Plants, Gardening and You." Offered by the University of Florida's Environmental Horticulture Department, this class is aimed for non-horticulture majors. In the past, I have been asked to speak to college classes on topics usually related to marketing, market research, and/or trends in the horticulture industry. This will be the first time I address a college class on a topic that probably relates more to America in Bloom than anything else in my classroom repertoire.

So, I soon will be on stage in front of 200 students who are taking this course as an elective because they need the general education credit and/or because they think they like plants. Since they are mostly from outside the College of Agricultural and Life Sciences, I am assuming most have only been casually connected to plants or gardening. If I'm lucky, it may be an active hobby for some, but industry demographics would suggest this is a hobby usually developed later in life than the age of the typical college student.

This will be only the second class session in the new semester. My guess is I will be transmitting some of the first information many of these students will hear about plants or gardening. For this course and for this class, I think it will be prudent for me to talk mostly about the "You" in the course title. I asked one of the young people with whom I work what he thought was on the minds of the typical college student today. Bill suggested thoughts relating to the environment and sustainability would be important. He noted community and how one might be able to contribute to or even give back to the community would be salient messages. Bill was looking forward. For students and other young people who have so much more of their lives yet to live, looking forward is important! So, again, I think it will be important to discuss people issues to get any points across.

As I contemplate this assignment, I am convinced my task will be easy. I can talk about many of society's ills – violence, eating disorders, productivity declines, pollution, and crime, and I will be able to tell these students proudly that I work in a field that helps to fight these troubles. I can talk about the challenges of community – finding common ground, focus, and purpose, and I can tell them about America in Bloom, a program that helps turn populations into real communities, developing a corps of volunteers working for the common good of all citizens. And I can ask them about their future – vocational or avocational directions, and I can steer them to our beautiful world of plants and gardening and all that plants can offer to make their lives and our world a better place.

Bolstering some of these points are two related studies that discuss the value of city parks. The first (June 2008) was commissioned by the Philadelphia Parks Alliance and conducted by The Trust for Public Land's Center for City Park Excellence. Titled "How Much Value Does the City of Philadelphia Receive from its Park and Recreation System?", this groundbreaking study involved economists and other scientists from several universities, government agencies, and other organizations. The conclusion: the returns from Philadelphia's parks to the city and its citizens yield "about 100 times the amount that the city spends on parks each year."

The report details the returns. Cited were factors affecting the city government and factors affecting citizens. For example, the city gained tax receipts from increased property values(0.95% of the imputed returns) and city tax receipts from increased tourism (0.27%). The city saved costs for stormwater management (0.31%), air pollution mitigation (0.08%), and the value of community cohesion (defined as the value gained by promoting relationship building and its resulting social capital, 0.45%). Citizens saved money for direct use (56.23%) and health (due to increased physical activity and reduced medical costs, 3.63%), and increased their collective wealth from increased property values due to park proximity (35.99%) and profit from tourism (2.10%). In total, over $1.9 billion was conservatively estimated as the annual value of the Philadelphia Park and Recreation System.

The second study (March 2009), also conducted by The Trust for Public Land's Center for City Park Excellence, extended the first study to include data from several other cities' park systems. "Measuring the Economic Value of a City Park System" noted that not every aspect of a city park system can be quantified nor its returns evaluated; neither the mental health value of a walk in the woods nor the value of carbon sequestration were offered as examples.

Reading through these reports, many opportunities for follow-up research were noted. Yet, these reports provide a first attempt at recognizing the financial returns achievable from relatively modest investments in public park space. As Philadelphia Mayor Michael Nutter concluded in the first study when asking the citizens to invest even more in their park system, "Philadelphia already has one of the best and biggest park systems in the nation...This report puts the reasons why in dollars and cents."

Granted, parks are only part of the urban landscape, but many of the same benefits can accrue to the city and its citizens from a planting of street trees, the beauty of flowering hanging baskets adorning lampposts, well-maintained shrubs and turf on the lawns of municipal buildings, or the flower beds in people's front yards. With the New Year and the planning for our ninth AIB contest, we have an exciting opportunity to testify to the returns of urban beautification. And what an exciting opportunity I have to carry this message to a college campus as we march into this new decade.

Reasons' Greetings

December 2009

Recently, a holiday letter arrived which ended with "Merry Christmas, Happy Hannukah, Happy Kwanzaa, and Reasons' Greetings!" While, at first glance, the "R" appeared to be a typo, the more this was pondered, the more intentional that "R" appeared. Indeed, life often races during the period between Thanksgiving and New Years Day, and seldom do we take the time to contemplate the many reasons to give thanks, to spend time with family and friends, and to consider the true meanings of the season.

America in Bloom has indeed been considering its strategic meaning of late. Our Board of Directors is in the midst of Strategic Planning, having spent an initial two days in late November to re-evaluate our mission statement and goals. And while we made some minor tweaks to the wording (see below), our mission has remained relatively unchanged. Yet to occur is the establishment of a list of strategies and tactics we will implement to achieve our goals – something we will be tackling between now and spring.

Strategic planning aside, in the spirit of the season, it might be appropriate to consider the reasons America in Bloom means so much to the cities that have truly embraced the program. Mayor after mayor has told us that the program turned their city into a real community. Yes, the flowers, trees, shrubs, turf, and groundcovers have enhanced the beauty of many shopping districts, Main Streets, city entrances, and the homes and businesses of citizens and merchants throughout their towns. And the enhanced beauty has often led to more shoppers, more tourists, more residents, higher property values, and a greater tax base.

Yet, even with all of these reasons, it is often the other issues that keep cities involved in the AIB program. Cities report a greater sense of pride among citizens. This is often demonstrated by less litter and graffiti (part of what AIB calls "tidiness"), a greater appreciation of the city's history and heritage, a greater awareness of the environmental impact of everything that occurs in the city, and closer working relationships that develop between the city government, businesses, civic organizations, and residents. Mayors often report developing "a real sense of community" as a result of their AIB efforts.

Along with the beauty and greater pride citizens take in their city, there are usually even more benefits. Scientific studies have shown lower crime rates, greater civility, and more productivity in the presence of green spaces than without. Students do better in school, as exemplified from greater attentiveness, higher grades, and less disruption in the classroom. Psychologically, young people have demonstrated greater self-discipline, and everyone deals more easily with the pressures of life's demands when vegetation and natural settings are part of the urban landscape. For research and articles on the benefits of plants visit AIB's Benefits of Plants resource page.

Of course, from the AIB perspective, one of the greatest reasons we need to contemplate the true meaning of the season is to thank our many volunteers who participate in the America in Bloom activities at the national and local levels. AIB is an all-volunteer organization, from the Board of Directors and our judges, all of whom serve without compensation, to the folks at the local level who get their hands dirty planting the flowers and plants that so enrich the lives of the citizens in participating cities. We truly owe each of you a great "pat on the back" and a hearty "THANK YOU" for all you do throughout the year.

So, there really are a lot of reasons to bring greetings this holiday season. And for all of the AIB family, have the merriest of holidays, the brightest of New Years, and the most rewarding fruits of your labors in 2010. We hope to see you and your city enrolled in the 2010 AIB contest. And if any of you have a few spare dollars at year's end, your tax deductible contributions will be greatly appreciated. America in Bloom remains a 501 (c)(3) non-profit organization and your contributions are deductible to the full extent of the law according to IRS regulations.

AIB's revised Mission Statement:

America in Bloom promotes nationwide beautification through education and community involvement by encouraging the use of flowers, plants, trees, and other environmental and lifestyle enhancements.

Introspection: The Year of Luxuries and Necessities
November 2009

The last year has certainly been tumultuous. Last November we elected a new president, and in the months leading up to that election, Americans were offered choices that had never before been presented in presidential campaigns. For many months prior, there had been a legitimate female contender for the presidential nomination, and in the end, there was another woman running as Vice President.

There was an African-American running for President on one of the major party's ticket. The choices for the top offices presented many Americans with difficult decisions, as we examined our personal biases and bigotries and weighed these against the candidates who we each thought offered the best ideas. For many, the self-examination asked whether we, as Americans, truly believed that "All men are created equal." Indeed, this line was first used in 1776 by Thomas Jefferson in the Declaration of Independence. It was later quoted by Abraham Lincoln in his 1863 Gettysburg Address. And Martin Luther King, Jr. used this in his "I have a dream" speech in 1963. Yet, on the eve of the 2008 election, Americans asked themselves whether they truly believed this line that had been used repeatedly throughout America's 232-year history. This serious introspection was not easy for many. Even with 24 hours left before the polls opened on the East Coast, polls indicated 14 percent of probable voters were still undecided.

As if that decision was not difficult enough, Americans learned a month later we were officially in a recession, one that was already a year old. Compounding the news was the unemployment forecast, which suggested that 1 in 10 Americans would likely be unemployed before the recession ended, an unfortunate statistic that has come true. In parts of the country unemployment is considerably higher.

Add to this the legions of Americans who are underemployed, those earning a paycheck in a field which is not commensurate with their training or experience, and those working reduced hours. Year-end bonuses did not materialize for many, and some have gone without customary pay raises. Home foreclosures are at record levels, and property values have plummeted in many locales. Americans are suddenly debating what is really important in their lives.

Lest one think the statistics are just numbers printed across a newspaper's page, it is important to think of the detail in individual terms. I have to find a new car dealership before my next oil change or needed repair, as the dealership I have used for over the last quarter century has closed its doors.

I also need to find a new clothing store, as the place I have purchased over 90 percent of my clothes for more than 20 years is no longer there. My favorite Italian restaurant has also gone out of business after 20 years. And the bank president down the street from where I live, with over 25 years of banking experience, was bagging groceries at the local grocery store the last time I saw him. In each of these cases, people I personally know are now unemployed or underemployed. Stress and fear are now parts of their lives. The crisis of confidence is an issue of personal reflection for many.

Certainly with unemployment and home foreclosures high and with mergers, bankruptcies, and those businesses ceasing operations in the forefront of thought, the general concern for many Americans is one of budgets. For many, the times have called for purse-string restraint wherever possible.

Cities, too, have faced financial strains, as unemployment has led to lower tax revenues when income, property, or sales taxes are part of the revenue stream. Especially in the hardest hit states, the prognosis for municipal budgets is bleak at best. What is a city to do? The answer for many cities has been to cut back non-essential services. But the debate centers on what is considered a luxury and necessity. Unfortunately, too often the discussion becomes a "black vs. white debate" based on personal bias and does not include seeking alternative "grey" ways to accomplish the same goals. Perhaps, if consulted, businesses, civic organizations, and individual citizens would step up to the plate to provide funding or the volunteer efforts needed, which may no longer be afforded as municipal services. Such times certainly call for creative thinking, negotiating, and personal outreach.

When considering the importance of certain expenditures, one naturally weighs costs vs. benefits. If flowers and plants are considered only for their aesthetic qualities, one might easily brand them luxuries that cannot be afforded. Yet, as regular readers of this column are aware, flowers, trees, sod, shrubs, and groundcovers offer a lot more than beauty. These horticultural wonders offer calmness, stress reduction, motivation, crime reduction, inspiration, self respect, attentiveness, pride, and many other lifestyle benefits critically important during stressful times.

Plants also can help mitigate urban climate extremes (including urban heat islands), can help ameliorate air, water, sewage and noise pollution, can help with flood and erosion control, can act as windbreaks, and can help control urban glare and reflection. Plants can help attract birds and other wildlife to the urban environment, can be used as a fun teaching tool for reading, writing, arithmetic, and biology, and can be used to help create a presence, whether marking the edge of or entrance to a city, one's personal space, a public space, a business district, or even helping with traffic flow. In the process, these plant packages also have learned to sequester carbon and make oxygen at the same time! Indeed, we need to have both active and passive relationships with plants, as we need to be around plants for the inspiration and spirituality they provide and to have plants around us for all of the utilitarian benefits they offer. For details on the scientific evidence relating to any of the plant attributes or benefits I mentioned, please visit "The Benefits of Plants" under Resources on the AIB website at www.americainbloom.org.

One of our America in Bloom judges, Marlborough Packard, a professor of historic preservation at the Savannah College of Art and Design, recently asked, "Would we think differently about the arts and horticulture if for every poem not written there was a heart attack, for every painting not painted there was an aneurism, and for every flower not planted there was a stroke?" Certainly we would! But even if the consequences are less dramatic, might I suggest that most Americans and, perhaps, even some in the horticulture industry, undervalue what plants can contribute to society.

As one might imagine, the recession has had varying consequences on particular horticultural subsectors, with horticultural businesses also sharing in the unfortunate business closure statistics. Some businesses have reported record years, but more have reported flat to declining sales, somewhat akin to how the local economies in which they market their products are performing. Those producing trees and shrubs, for the most part, have fortunes at least partly tied to new construction and the sales of new or newly acquired homes or business properties.

Landscapers focusing on maintenance seem relatively unscathed, especially if the focus is on commercial properties, while those focused on new installations generally have struggled. Parts of the sod and groundcover subsectors are also tied to building construction, though some are tied to recreational installations like parks and golf courses; here, too, recessionary pain has been felt. For those producing floriculture products, the jury is still out, as some have reported record years, while others have seen sales reduced. The story for retailers seems as mixed as the weather, as firms even in close proximity to one another have had very different seasons, perhaps, dependent on how they are perceived for product innovation and selection, customer service, promotion, or other marketing variables.

Certainly for those who have recognized the benefits of horticultural products, the essential importance of a program like America in Bloom is apparent. Indeed, many cities have announced enhanced planting programs in this last year, even in these challenging times, for they realize the power of plants in the urban environment. We thank you for making your cities more beautiful and for adopting the many ancillary benefits plants offer alongside the aesthetics, for these benefits are truly needed now more than ever. We thank you for recognizing the power of volunteerism and for the strength it can offer in turning your cities and towns into real communities. And we thank you all for planting pride in your communities and in the hearts of your citizens.

Random Thoughts From Hershey, Pennsylvania

October 2009

During the almost four days I spent in Hershey, Pennsylvania, earlier this month for the America in Bloom Symposium and Awards Program, my mind kept bouncing from thought to thought. During past visits, I might have blamed that on the smell of chocolate, but I really didn't detect the aroma of chocolate in the air during this trip. I have been to Hershey at least "umpteen" if not 20-some times previously, but it had been over 35 years since I last visited. (As much travelling as I do, I'm not old enough to have been somewhere about 20 times and to not have been there in over 35 years.)

Thought 1. The days in Hershey were filled. From judges training, to seminars, to awards programs, to an AIB Board of Directors meeting, I kept quite busy. Still, there was time to meet old friends and make new ones from cities that believe in what America in Bloom is trying to accomplish. We had 25 cities participate in this year's program, two of which experienced our new "participant-only" non-competitive options. But we had folks from 68 cities in all at the symposium. Sure, this tally included our judges, staff, and board members, but it also included folks just wanting to learn more about what AIB has to offer.

Thought 2. Folks remain very passionate about their towns. We had people repeatedly stand up to promote their city's "brag books," so that others could see what they had accomplished. We had people who really wanted to compare notes of how they tackled a certain issue to see if others might offer a better solution. We had people who wanted to make sure the judges had seen this or that when visiting their cities, as if a last-minute mention might still help improve their score. And we had people recognized for their leadership qualities, as we presented all of our nominees and the first winner of the John R. Holmes III Community Champion Award. Congratulations to Rick Webb of Logan, Ohio, for this award and for all you do for the city.

Thought 3. Everyone is trying to make life simpler, as is AIB. Our contest committee is developing a template for cities to use to report on their activities across all eight judging criteria and the three constituent groups. We recognize the 24 cells in our judging grid can seem daunting to some, but our hope is this City Profile template will help cities organize their accomplishments, making it easier for both cities and judges to communicate about the pertinent pieces of what has been done as part of the AIB effort. Those cities that still want to tackle a larger "brag book" to record a more thorough accounting of the details are welcome to do so.

Thought 4. Our judges really are a very dedicated group of volunteers. They do their best to capture the essence of a competing city and yet communicate some valuable ideas they've learned in another city which might help the experience for the citizens in the city they are now judging. This is not easy work. Not all suggestions will fit every city. And some cities are better able to incorporate such suggestions than others.

Thought 5. There is advantage to participating over and over again in the AIB program. Our judges have different backgrounds, and they see each city in a different light. With each contest, your city receives a new and equally valid opinion from each new pair of judges who visit. The possible challenge is you may not score quite as well from a subsequent judging. Yet, the new evaluation is just as pertinent as the old, as each is given at a point in time as seen through different eyes. (This is not dissimilar to what may happen to an Olympic athlete on a different day, with different judges, and with possibly different competitors.) The truly outstanding city is the one that shines consistently for each new visitor time after time. It is only from repeated judging that a city can learn if a city's visitor experience is sustained over and over again.

During the judges' training, our Judge Coordinator, Jack Clasen, told of a city visited this summer in Ireland, which he judged in the International Competition. (AIB participates in this challenge as well, pitting our best winning cities against those from similar programs in Canada, Europe, and Asia.) This city had competed for 30 years straight in the Tidy Towns of Ireland program, but they have only won four times. I wondered what makes a city participate so religiously, especially knowing their historical odds of winning are outpaced by their odds of not taking home the trophy. As I thought about this, it occurred to me the city may feel the need to constantly improve, knowing the bar was being raised by surrounding towns every year. I also wondered if Tidy Towns of Ireland was viewed by this city as a type of ritual akin to our spring cleaning. We know our houses seem to get dirty, even while we're away on vacation, but we go through our spring cleaning procedures habitually as a rite of spring just to stay even. In the end, I'm guessing the city truly wants the feedback received in their evaluations. It can be quite satisfying knowing how visitors view what you have to offer, irrespective of the scores.

Thought 6. The town of Hershey is gorgeous! Nestled into the rolling hills of rural central Pennsylvania, Milton Hershey built this town, located in the Derry Township, to house his chocolate factory. At the same time, Mr. Hershey, an entrepreneur who had had mixed luck with previous ventures, recognized that a city had to be more than just a place to house a factory and the homes of his workers. He built cultural and recreational facilities for the townspeople. He built roads but also invested in mass transportation. And he also built gardens. The famed Hershey Rose Gardens were later transformed into the Hershey Gardens, but even the grounds of Hershey's personal residence, up on the hill overlooking the factory, were open for the public to visit.

Hershey also knew the value of education and its ability to transform the fortunes of the individual. He and his wife founded the Milton Hershey School, which still today, 100 years after its founding, provides a free education to any of the more than 1,000 students enrolled. The school especially helps the less fortunate, those from single parent households, broken homes, and those for which this type of a boarding school is often viewed as a life-saving improvement over their home situation. Hershey included horticulture in the curriculum for all students, and while that has changed a bit, there still are greenhouses on campus used by students in the elementary and middle school years.

The city of Hershey still includes some of the best examples of beautiful landscaping for a city of its size in America. Hanging baskets, planters, flower beds, and gardens are everywhere. Beautiful old trees dot the landscape. The landscaping at the Hotel Hershey includes some of the most dramatic examples of bedding plant use I have seen at a hotel in a long time. At one point, I counted five tiers of window boxes and hanging baskets moving up the façade of the hotel's front entryway and terraces.

Thought 7. America in Bloom is on a roll. While we do not have plans for next year's Symposium quite finalized, rest assured, we will be having a contest and a very special Symposium. Details will be announced as soon as negotiations with facilities are completed. The Board of Directors was very pleased with the turnout of this year's Symposium, especially considering the economic climate our country is facing. A sentiment heard over and over again was the need to keep people both engaged with and around horticulture (active) and to have horticulture around people (passive) during these stressful times. Urban beautification can certainly play a part in keeping tensions calmed, crime low, and productivity high. Urban beautification can help stimulate a local economy, help direct visitors to a destination, add to property values, and keep the living and working environments pleasant for all to enjoy. In these trying times, now more than ever, we need to keep involved with America in Bloom projects all across the country.

On behalf of the entire AIB Board of Directors, I want to thank everyone who participated in the Hershey Symposium. It truly was sweet. And I want to thank everyone who participated in an AIB effort in your city or town this year. Enrollment is now open for next year's contest, and it's our hope that each city will be back again and also encouraging your neighboring cities to join the AIB program. For those mayors, city managers, or city councilmen attending the National League of Cities' Congress of Cities in San Antonio next month, please be sure to stop by the America in Bloom booth to say hello, and please consider bringing a city official from another city with you, so we can plant a seed. Together, we can help plant so much pride in cities and towns across America.

Leaders All, Champions Everyone

September 2009

As most of the regular readers of the AIB e-newsletter already know, America in Bloom established the John R. Holmes III Community Champion Award in memory of our late Board member and Secretary/Treasurer. As a member of the award subcommittee I recently reviewed the over 30 nominations received for our first annual Community Champion Award, and received a glimpse of the nomination characteristics each of the worthy nominees possess. The winner will be announced Saturday, October 3, during the AIB Symposium and Award Ceremony in Hershey, Pennsylvania.

John Holmes was a close friend during the seven years I knew him. He often introduced himself as "my brother of a another mother." He obviously had a sense of humor to be sure, and we enjoyed a quality relationship that only close friends have. We could laugh together, but we could also debate and still remain friends. I believe John was often misunderstood by many of those with whom he had contact who did not take the time to really get to know him. In his often quiet way, John usually had a vision on many issues, and he worked toward achieving his targeted goals.

In similar fashion, reading the words offered by the nominators makes me believe that most cities have their champions. Sometimes the champions are politicians or other city employees. Sometimes they are business or civic leaders. Some might be residents wanting to make a difference. Often they are the quiet leaders that just help to get things done, always targeting the goal of what's best for the community. The characteristics listed for the nominees exhibited some similarities, but they were also as varied as those individuals who offered the nominations. In a few instances, a certain nominee received multiple nominations, and these descriptions sometimes spoke quite differently about the same individual. Such variety might be the nature of individual impressions, individual interactions, or just the result of limiting essays to 500 words.

Our subcommittee was awed by a number of points. First, we felt these nominees were all worthy candidates. We struggled to agree about the most important characteristics for evaluating the candidates. In the end, we agreed that all were champions, each worthy of being nominated for the strength they exhibited in leading their cities toward accomplishing their AIB goals. AIB wants to salute every nominee, and we hope all will be able to attend the symposium in Hershey so that we may acknowledge your efforts in person.

Secondly, we debated the merits of the nomination process itself. Obviously, literary eloquence played a role. We could only judge the essays as submitted, but it was clear some authors had more experience writing nominations than others. In evaluating the essays, we tried to sift through the writing styles and evaluate what was said about each candidate. Did additional essays on the same candidate help the nominee? We did not always agree on this, probably because we could not generalize on their merits.

So, what characteristics did these champions possess? We read testimony of hard work, folks who rolled up their sleeves and worked alongside other volunteers. These champions got their hands dirty, literally! Our champions also exhibited passion and often planted their passion into the hearts of fellow volunteers. Champions were said to have vision, strength of character, and conviction. They were successful in turning their visions into reality. Some of these visions related to flowers and plants, some related to fundraising goals, some related to amassing volunteers to get the work completed. And some related to the ultimate goal of bringing the community together. Tallies of trees transplanted, hanging baskets hung, planters positioned, or hours volunteered were offered as proof.

The words leader and leadership were used, often in conjunction with getting the job done, with responsibilities taken, or with "organizing the troops." Communication skills, dedication, enthusiasm, and generosity were suggested attributes as well. Nominees were said to be positive people, to be positive role models, to have positive attitudes, and to have positive work ethics. Though not always described, per se, our subcommittee got the sense that most of these nominees truly believed in their cities. Their efforts seemed motivated by more than the desire to just get the job done, by more than the need to plant some flowers, trees, shrubs or sod, and by more than the need to win. Even when the nominee was a mayor, a city manager, or other city employee, one got the sense that the nominee truly believed in the city and what their city was or could be; after all, it was still "their city," and they still were proud of what had been accomplished. Essays often described the results of the nominee's efforts, in terms of enhanced beautification, more tidy neighborhoods, and citizenry with greater environmental awareness, better appreciation for horticulture, or even the town's history.

Yet, throughout these essays, one got the sense that our nominees displayed a constancy of purpose, the need to achieve the stated goals, the need to help their city come together as a real community and shine. Truly, our nominees want to help plant pride in their communities. And for this kind of dedication, I believe John Holmes would have been proud to meet these champions and to have any one of these candidates selected as the Community Champion award winner. Congratulations, again, to all nominees! You are all winners and recognized as leaders. Every one of you is a champion!

The Sense of Wonder

January 2009

"A child's world is fresh and new and beautiful, full of wonder and excitement. It is our misfortune that for most of us that clear-eyed vision, that true instinct for what is beautiful and awe-inspiring, is dimmed and even lost before we reach adulthood ...."

So wrote Rachel Carson in her last book, <u>The Sense of Wonder</u> (Harper Collins Publishers, 1998). Perhaps, best know for <u>Silent Spring</u>, the book many suggest spawned environmental awareness, Rachel Carson wrote this book, published posthumously, in which she encouraged parents to take their children for a walk in the woods. Her hypothesis was that children exposed to nature at an early age would develop a sense of wonder about the world around them, about ecosystems, and about each creature's interdependence upon others. More importantly, this sense of wonder was essential for a gratifying life. And for Rachel Carson, personally, this walk in the woods was essential for both the woods' and man's survival.

"If a child is to keep alive his inborn sense of wonder without any such gift from the fairies, he needs the companionship of at least one adult who can share it, rediscovering with him the joy, excitement and mystery of the world we live in."

For Carson, the adult was an important transfer agent. He or she would lend both meaning and importance to the world around the child. Walking together through the woods, however, would consciously impact both parties, the child and the chaperone.

The holiday season often brings visions of amazement for the young. They debate what might be in the boxes with the colorful wrapping and the pretty bows. They wonder how someone the size of the mall Santa can make it down the small opening of the fireplace chimney. Those living in homes without fireplaces ask if they'll get any presents at all. And with these questions answered, the awe of the holiday often dissipates within a few days if not a few hours of the presents' unveilings.

Yet, Carson's contention was that Nature presents enough awe to last a lifetime, if we would only pause to observe it with all of the senses.

"I sincerely believe that for the child, and for the parent seeking to guide him, it is not half so important to know as to feel. If facts are the seeds that later produce knowledge and wisdom, then the emotions and the impressions of the senses are the fertile soil in which the seeds must grow."

I hope you might find the time to take a walk in the woods. Witness nature in action. Witness the quiet of the woods, even when it is full of life. Witness the diversity of life forms, of shapes and sizes. Witness the beauty of nature in all her glory. It truly can be as exhilarating as having visions of sugar plums. And with luck, the walk in the woods can help extend that sense of wonder to last a lifetime!

Lessons from a Northern Think Tank

July 2008

"I'd like to say we plant all these flowers and plants, just because I like flowers and plants, but frankly, I can't sell City Council on all these expenditures just because I like flowers."

That's how Mayor Richard Daley opened his keynote address at the 2003 America in Bloom Symposium, held in Chicago, Illinois, after Chicago took the prize in the large city category in 2002, our first AIB contest year. Daley continued this theme, as if uninterrupted by time, during an office visit I made to Chicago's City Hall a few years later.

"So, we cite all of the other reasons people should plant flowers and trees and shrubs and lawns that go beyond the beauty, to reasons explaining why the horticulture makes Chicago a better place to live."

A recently reviewed 64-page report from the George Morris Centre, Canada's so-called "Independent Agri-Food Think Tank," reminded me of the words Mayor Daley used. Titled "Literature Review of Documented Health and Environmental Benefits Derived from Ornamental Horticulture Products - Final Report," this March 2007 document concludes that a review of literature "demonstrated that ornamental horticulture has a wider suite of benefits than expected. Plants can provide multiple benefits in terms of the economy, environment and human lifestyles."

The report cited economic benefits from reducing heating and cooling costs, improving property values, improving privacy and security, reducing maintenance costs, and deriving new economic benefits from parks, sporting facilities, and increased tourism. Specifically, the report cited several studies which showed that vegetation can provide energy savings and can help cool the air. Landscaping added to property values in another series of cited works. One study suggested that by spending 5% of a home's value on the installation of quality low-maintenance landscaping, resale values increased by 15%, which translated into a 150% return on the landscaping investment. A survey of one community found that 74% of the public preferred to patronize commercial establishments where the structures and parking lots had landscaping. In another study, 86% of real estate appraisers agreed that landscaping added to the value of commercial real estate, and 92% agreed that landscaping increased the sales appeal. Occupancy rates were higher in rental properties with landscape amenities, too.

Environmental benefits included moderating urban climate extremes; mitigating urban heat islands; ameliorating air, soil, water, sewage and wastewater pollution; controlling floods and erosion; reducing weather impacts through the use of windbreaks and shelterbelts; reducing noise pollution; assisting in control of visual glare and reflection; and attracting birds and other wildlife. Perhaps, most importantly, ornamental horticultural plants have the ability to sequester carbon and produce oxygen. Specifically, the report cited studies showing that two mature trees or a 2,500 square foot lawn each can produce enough oxygen for a family of four each year.

Identified lifestyle benefits included stress reduction; improved productivity; quicker hospital recoveries; horticultural therapy to improve mind, body and spirit; medicinal uses; improved quality of life and life satisfaction; improved attention and concentration for children; reduction of aggression and violence; space for recreation; and the creation of pride in communities. In one often-cited study, patients assigned to hospital rooms with a view looking out on natural scenes had shorter postoperative hospital stays. However, a lesser-known study with similar results discussed window views of nature in prisons for inmates; those with greener views reported lower frequencies of prisoner stress symptoms. In another study of urbanized inner-city public housing, residents living in relatively landscape-barren buildings reported more aggression than did their counterparts living in buildings with relatively greener landscapes; mental fatigue was also higher for residents living in relatively landscape-barren buildings, and aggression accompanied mental fatigue. This study also concluded that although large central or regional parks were important components of urban design, having nature at almost every doorstep is important. Separately, the same researchers found that the greener a building's surroundings, the fewer crimes were reported for both property crimes and violent crimes. In yet another study, ornamental plants contributed not only beauty, but also pride that people had in their cities, towns or dwellings; the pride and development of community was seen especially when gardening was done on a collective basis by the residents of a community.

The report also noted that the industry itself contributed directly to the economy in a number of ways. First there is employment in both the production and the service sectors related to supplying consumers with horticultural products and value-added services. In many economies, the ornamental horticultural products become a source of tax revenues, and often the only agricultural products that are taxed, as sales taxes are often not collected on food. The floricultural and nursery products that make up this ornamental horticulture industry often are traded globally, so import and export services and issues relating to the balance of trade are also considerations.

This report is available on the AIB website's list of resources under "the benefits of plants." Please feel to download it, and please do read it. In the meantime, just remember that the plant you so love for its beauty may be contributing more than a smile to your life. Indeed, it may be contributing in so many other ways.

The Anatomy of Writer's Block

Super Bowl XLII and Spring Training Camp
March, 2008

I knew the message I wanted to send. I thought everyone could relate to the first part if they had been among the 90 million Americans who had watched Super Bowl XLII or among the many millions more that had seen articles, read Internet blogs, saw the television news or video clips and/or heard anyone commenting on the commercials aired during the broadcast. I just struggled with how to connect this with the second part of the message I wanted to deliver.

On Sunday, February 3, over 90 million Americans watched Super Bowl XLII. Aside from the fantastic game on the field, much of the discussion of the day surrounded the 60 commercial spots seen during the game's broadcast. It seemed by game's end, there was almost as much talk about which company sponsored the most memorable commercial as there was about the New York Giants upset win over the New England Patriots. Indeed, the $2.7 million charged for a 30-second commercial may seem trivial if an advertiser's product or service was still a topic of conversation on the Monday following the game. Such is the added value of word-of-mouth advertising.

America in Bloom also benefits from word of-mouth conversations about the program benefits offered to participating cities and towns. Indeed, if one looks at the map of cities registered in the first seven editions of our contest, there is no doubt that several clusters are visible across the country. We often hear of the word-of-mouth communication that has fostered a city to consider the program after a neighboring city had entered the contest. Clusters in Northwest Ohio are the most evident, but clusters also exist in Southwest Ohio, Southern Indiana, and Northeastern Illinois. Smaller clusters appear in New England, Southern California, Northwest Arkansas and elsewhere.

I thought I was able to link the benefits of word-of-mouth advertising from the Super Bowl to America in Bloom successfully enough. I was ready to make the case for helping to create the buzz.

But there is a major difference between the buzz created from Super Bowl commercials and that created by America in Bloom. That difference certainly can be measured in dollars, but it also can be measured in time. The Super Bowl lasted for part of the afternoon and evening of February 3. America in Bloom's reach, which is now estimated to "touch" millions of people per year who are exposed to some form of AIB media coverage, has taken just over six years to achieve.

One might ask, "Which is better, the exposure to 90 million Americans in an afternoon and evening or the exposure to millions of Americans per year?" Of course the correct answer largely depends upon the lasting effects of the exposure. Media considerations aside, it might be argued that the benefits AIB participation bring to a city have a much more lasting effect. But as with advertising, a more pertinent question might be, "To what extent might we be able to increase the reach even more?" Super Bowl advertisers often use humor to increase the recall of an ad. For America in Bloom, a large part of our success has to be the buzz that occurs when cities have positive experiences and when the lives of their residents are affected. If successful municipalities reach out to neighboring cities and towns and/or when neighboring citizens and townspeople see the changes that occur in a city in their midst and seek out the impetus of that change, the reach becomes all the more powerful.

I next struggled to link the discussion to baseball, my hardest challenge in this piece thus far. I knew where I wanted the article to go, and where I wanted it to end up -- home plate. The question was how to connect the two. As with football, baseball offers some insights from which we can learn. No single baseball game brings in the ad revenue of football's Super Bowl. Yet, baseball's long schedule and the daily effort required throughout the season can both serve as needed metaphors to help drive home points that needed to be made.

Now, less than two weeks after the Super Bowl, baseball pitchers have already begun to report to spring training camps. Remaining players are just a day or two behind. Tentative rosters will be finalized quickly. Exhibition games will soon begin. In almost no time, fans will be able to appreciate the excitement of "Play ball!" as another game, indeed as another long regular baseball season, begins in early April.

Come September, baseball's moment in the national spotlight will shine as the playoffs and then another World Series are played. Unlike the Super Bowl, with baseball's season finale, two teams come together to play at least four, and possibly seven games. The season is long. The finale may seem even longer. The winner inevitably will be the team that is best able to stay in shape, the team that is best able to muster the wins, day in and day out.

The repetition of the nine-inning sets we call a normal baseball game, played day after day over a period of more than six months, for over 160 games even before the playoffs begin, is, perhaps, more akin to the repetition needed for effective promotion. Much of the advertising associated with baseball is more local in nature, in part because relatively few games are nationally broadcast. And even though the many teams' relative fortunes are revealed daily in the standings printed during the season in newspapers coast-to-coast, the bulk of the publicity any one team gets might comes from word-of-mouth discussions around water coolers or other venues in the local market and surrounding areas.

Such is the nature of America in Bloom's achievement. We need the "water-cooler chatter" about the benefits to community. We need the long and continuous growth that occurs with each success, one city at a time. We need to have everybody swinging the bats to hear the roars from the crowds. And we need each and every participant to share their AIB stories with neighboring communities, so that good word-of-mouth communication can attract even more fans to the game. We'd certainly like to hit a home run from time to time, but base hits can also accrue just as many wins. We just have to keep swinging those bats in order to cross home plate!

Environmental Awareness: Oxygen—
The Original Greenhouse Gas

February 2008

About 20 years ago, I saw the first reference to the term "greenhouse gas," used in a pejorative tone. All references seen earlier had referred to "ozone depleting gases which contributed to the so-called greenhouse effect." Even then, I knew the writer's "shortcut" was not going to be good for the horticulture industry.

My first reaction was to contact one of our industry's Washington, DC-based trade organizations, which for years had been a watchdog looking out for industry interests. And for a number of years, the organization sent out letters to offending journalists talking about "greenhouse gases" to try to influence the verbiage used. Alas, the term "greenhouse gas" is much more prevalent today than any references to "the greenhouse effect."

Certainly, the ultimate significance to the horticulture industry of the shortened "greenhouse gas" expression, if any, can only be imagined. But the story told by Dr. Will Carlson, Extension Floriculturist (retired) at Michigan State University, perhaps, best illustrates the potential impact:

I was talking to an official in a Michigan town about getting approval for one of my grower constituents to build a new greenhouse. The official told me there was no way he could support the construction. When I asked why, he replied, "I can't come out in favor of anything for the industry responsible for greenhouse gases."

"The truth is the real greenhouse gas is oxygen, that by-product of photosynthesis. Plants take in carbon dioxide, one of the contributors to the so-called 'greenhouse effect,' and during photosynthesis, plants combine the CO_2 with water to produce oxygen," I countered. As I left the official's office, my head was shaking, partly in disbelief and partly from concern.

Over the many years since, the lexicon used seems to have totally disguised the truth about this so-called "greenhouse effect." Yet, it is also obvious that not everything the horticulture industry has done to improve efficiency is as good for the environment as the plants' oxygen output. While the beauty the horticulture industry offers has certainly grown in scope thanks to the modern methods and tools used to breed, produce and market its products, some of those very methods must now be re-examined to determine whether they provide the best sustainable approach for both the industry and the environment. Certainly, the same could be said for almost all agricultural subsectors.

Even as this self-examination continues, it is critically important that society continues to support all of agriculture including the horticultural subsectors and products. Certainly, we want to continue to eat and clothe our bodies, and we also should be able to nourish our souls with the beauty that flowers, trees, shrubs, turf and groundcovers offer. Even though we may need to reconsider some of the methods used to be sure certain environmental factors are included in the production equations, the U.S. food and fiber supply is undoubtedly the best there is. Certain floricultural, turf and nursery production practices must be reconsidered, as well. During this reassessment process, it is essential that the entire agricultural industry be sustained along with the environment, for it is only through industry growth that the necessary investments can be made for the environmental challenges to be addressed.

Over time, horticulture (which has always dealt with plants "hands on") has been able to contribute many scientific advances to the rest of agriculture and society due in part to practitioners' intimate relationships with the plants they produce. Advances such as tissue culture, work first done on orchids, has led to the entire field of biotechnology, which is now unlocking the doors of DNA genomic research. This will ultimately solve many of the mysteries of both growth and diseases for plants, animals and people. Drip irrigation on greenhouse benches has led to similar field applications, which are conserving scarce water resources throughout many arid regions of the world. And evaporative cooling first used in greenhouses has been adapted for use in livestock facilities, which has led to increased yields as animals remain more comfortable.

The list of benefits to society goes on from here, but this list will ultimately include more answers needed for environmental improvement. We already know that plants can aid in remediation at water treatment plants or at other sites with in-ground toxic wastes. Greenhouse production techniques for flower and vegetable seedlings have been adapted by the lumber industry to make forest production of timber nearly sustainable. The turf industry has developed lawn blends that use less water and fertilizer and may require less mowing in certain instances. And yes, we already have a number of U.S. floricultural industry greenhouses lining up for sustainable certification, a practice that has been implemented in parts of Europe for over a dozen years and has only recently been considered in the U.S. and other parts of the world.

Similarly, a number of progressive cities have added initiatives relating to recycling, tree plantings, green roofs, and the like to make the urban environment more pleasant. Some of these programs have near-term consequences, while others focus more on the distant future. Recycling efforts attempt to reduce the stream of wastes entering landfills and, perhaps, find alternative uses for what were previously buried remnants. So-called "green belts" surrounding highways or even whole cities attempt to tackle automobile exhaust and smog, and some programs utilizing alternative fuels for city fleets aim to eliminate some of the fumes altogether. Green roofs aid in conserving heat in winter and ameliorate the need for cooling in summer, something especially noticeable in inner-city environments, just as "green parking lots" reduce water runoff and contamination of urban water supplies. Urban beautification also contributes here, if only to attract residents and businesses to city centers, which can ultimately provide more concentrated opportunities for serving consumers in a more efficient economic setting.

For these reasons and more, America in Bloom incorporated environmental awareness into its judging criteria from the beginning, and we must continue to share information in this area. Horticulture is certainly being examined for its overall impact on the environment, and horticulture, which is defined as "intensive agriculture," remains an easy target for reporters, who always seem to have exposés near floral-giving holidays. They often describe our industry as using more inputs per acre than any other type of agricultural production but neglect to report that the industry also yields many more times the output per acre and does it with far fewer acres than other agricultural production models. In fact, we truly should be comforted in knowing more is being invested by internal investigators working to improve the environmental impact statements for industry production than is being spent by external pundits putting horticulture under editorial microscopes.

No doubt, there certainly is a way to go. Yet, by acquainting more of America with the beauty our industry offers and letting more Americans experience the benefits of plants first-hand, we can all breathe both a sigh of relief, as well as that original greenhouse gas, oxygen.

Special Year-End President's Message

A Holiday Story: Of Missions, Chimpanzees, Cities and Gardening
December, 2007

Seven years ago, when America in Bloom first was a glimmer in the eyes of some folks in the horticulture industry, the program was viewed as a possible way to promote the industry. Afterall, similar programs had flourished for decades in several European countries where urban beautification had become part of the culture. And while industry promotion has always been part of the thinking of the Board of Directors and the many in the horticulture industry that support the program, there was an almost immediate recognition that AIB was also very good for the communities that embraced the program. Many have heard me say that "America in Bloom is a community enhancement program 'masquerading' as a beautification contest." This line is particularly effective when trying to get the attention of a mayor, a member of a city council, an executive from a Chamber of Commerce, or another civic leader.

What is particularly pleasing for me when I talk about America in Bloom is that I can speak to all three aspects of AIB's goals, industry promotion, community enhancement, and, perhaps, most simplistically, about city beautification, with one voice, as the goals overlap and support each other. Certainly, the presence of flowers, trees, shrubs and well-maintained turf and groundcovers can add beauty to any scene. Plant people tend to be very passionate about their products, in general, but they're also used to connecting flowers and plants to people's everyday living and life events, literally from birth to the altar to the home and to the grave. Been to a florist lately?

But horticulture has also been shown to improve the quality of life on a scale grander than just for the individual. The Resource List on AIB's website (www.americainbloom.org) under "Participate" includes a number of studies which serve as testimony to the fact that the presence of green spaces improves the quality of life of nearby residents. One such study, conducted by the University of Illinois in Chicago's public housing projects (www.herl.uiuc.edu), found reduced crime, better grades for students, and fewer reports of attention deficit disorder were among the results for residents when they were exposed to green spaces, this in contrast with other residents of identical housing that was not landscaped. Ironically, this very study was just cited by primatologist and anthropologist Jane Goodall in an interview in the third 40th anniversary issue of Rolling Stone magazine (November 15, 2007). In citing the study, Dr. Goodall, who studied the social interactions of chimpanzees in East Africa, noted, "Kids need to be in nature. We need it for our psychological development. We're not created to live in blocks of cement with cement underfoot."

Chimpanzees aside, flowers, shrubs, trees and turf often serve as the only bits of nature in many urban environments. Nature must be shared both with our children and with those more mature, to help all keep life in perspective in the "concrete jungle." These little bits of nature might, in fact, help to expose folks of all ages to some of the realities about the planet as a whole, a concern that seems to be gaining momentum these days, even if it is not completely understood. As consumers more and more seem to be asking about the quality of their food, their water, and the air they breathe, it becomes important to share a little bit of agricultural reality with them, so they become exposed to what it takes to grow a flower, a plant, a lawn or a tree. When the AIB program gets adopted by a city, a little bit of horticulture often gets introduced into school curricula. Similar program additions often get added to the agendas of scout troops, civic organizations, and other institutions, including that of the city government itself. This can have profound effects on this and the next generation's understanding of agriculture, the environment, and the quality of that world in which we live.

Last month, I was once again privileged to represent America in Bloom at the National League of Cities' annual Congress of Cities event, held this year in New Orleans, LA. While there, I was able to see parts of the devastation of Hurricanes Katrina and Rita, but I also viewed part of the rebuilding process and the major parts of the city left virtually untouched by the storms. No doubt, some parts of town have a long way to go in the rebuilding process, but a certain calm pervades even here, as the grass is green and the stately live oaks rein over the neighborhoods, both living essentially undeterred by the flooding. Happily, AIB Board Member Katy Moss Warner and I were able to share the AIB story during personal conversations with mayors and city council members from over 70 cities from all across the country during the Congress. This followed a trip in August to the American Chamber of Commerce Executives Annual Conference in Sacramento, CA; here, AIB volunteer staffer Alicia Wells and I had the chance to talk to many Chamber executives about our program. At both of these events, our AIB story resonated with most everyone with whom we spoke, as almost everyone asked for more information and agreed to be added to our e-newsletter mailing list.

Events like attending the National League of Cities and the American Chamber of Commerce Executives annual meetings are AIB's major attempts to reach out to more and more cities to become part of our contest in particular, but also to embrace our philosophy of adding horticulture to their cityscapes. City officials do "get it" and recognize that enhancing their cities will broaden the appeal for residents, for shoppers, and for tourists. They recognize that horticulture can add to property values. Whether or not they immediately recognize the added benefits for the quality of life of the residents in general might be debated. However, with time, these civic leaders also come to recognize these attributes; there is just too much scientific data to refute such a finding. And for the cities that remain committed to the program over time, we've been told that a transformation has been effected that results in a real change in community spirit and civic pride. A sustained grass roots cooperative attitude results, which helps to permanently change the culture of a community for the better.

Perhaps, ironically, with all that horticulture has going for it in terms of lifestyle and urban enhancement, we in the industry find ourselves increasingly discussing a two-part trend which will affect both the cities across America and the horticultural businesses that serve them:

On the one hand, people continue to report enjoying flowers and plants in their environs, and increasingly, people are paying premiums to live near well-landscaped parks; this has been reported in real-estate study after study, from coast to coast.

On the other hand, folks increasingly cite a lack of time as a reason why their own gardening efforts have declined.

In a just-released study from the National Gardening Association of Burlington, VT, we learn that Americans are now paying more for residential lawn and garden services than they are spending to do these activities on their own.

So, what does this mean? In this season of giving, I think it is important to pause to understand the opportunities that America in Bloom offers. For civic leaders, AIB offers the opportunity to enhance the lives of your residents. AIB programs in city after city have certainly added to the beauty. But AIB has also helped cities to form real communities, as folks work together in ways they have never before experienced: citizens, working alongside civic, business and municipal leaders taking an active role in landscaping, both figuratively and literally, their city for the future.

For folks in the horticulture industry, I think it is important to realize not only the impact our products are having on residents, but also the impact that societal trends are having on the industry. In a day and age when folks increasingly report no longer having enough time to commit to their own gardens, it is important that we help cities spread the horticultural passion we all have, for we know the power that flowers and plants can have on the human soul. And urban landscaping might just be good for the health of the industry in the process.

Have a Very Merry Holiday Season and a Beautiful 2008!

AIB Board Members 2014

Charlie Hall, Ph.D. President
Katy Moss Warner
  Vice President
Michael V. Geary
  Secretary/Treasurer
Marvin Miller
  Past President
Evelyn Alemanni
  Chair, External Relations
Jack Clasen
  Chair, Contest Committee
Bobby Barnitz
Kurt Becker
Tony Ferrara
Lela Kelly
Edith Makra
Stan Pohmer
Laura Kunkle
  Executive Director

AIB Judges 2014

Jack Clasen
  Chair, Contest Committee
Evelyn Alemanni
Sue Amatangelo
Billy Butterfield
Diane Clasen
Linda Cromer
Bill Hahn
Ed Hooker III
Dwight Lund
Marlborough B. Packard
Stephen Pategas
Leslie Pittenger
Alex Pearl
Bruce Riggs
Melanie Riggs
Karin Rindal
Susie Stratton
Jim Sutton
Barbara Vincentson
Katy Moss Warner
Diana K. Weiner

To learn more about America in Bloom

please visit

www.americainbloom.org

Contact us at aib@americainbloom.org

America in Bloom
2130 Stella Ct.
Columbus, OH 43215

www.ingramcontent.com/pod-product-compliance
Lightning Source LLC
Chambersburg PA
CBHW071358310526
45789CB00020B/520